OPERATION CHINA

OPERATION CHINA

From Strategy to Execution

Jimmy Hexter
Jonathan Woetzel

Harvard Business School Press
Boston, Massachusetts

Copyright 2007 McKinsey & Company, Inc.
All rights reserved
Printed in the United States of America
11 10 09 08   5 4 3 2

Library of Congress Cataloging-in-Publication Data

Hexter, Jimmy.
    Operation China: from strategy to execution / Jimmy Hexter, Jonathan
Woetzel.
        p.   cm.
    Includes bibliographical references and index.
    ISBN-13: 978-1-4221-1696-8 (hardcover: alk. paper)
    ISBN-10: 1-4221-1696-4
    1. International business enterprises—China—Management. I. Woetzel,
Jonathan. II. Title.
    HD62.4.H48 2007
    658'.0490951—dc22

                                                              2007021750

The paper used in this publication meets the requirements of the American
National Standard for Permanence of Paper for Publications and Documents
in Libraries and Archives Z39.48-1992.

CONTENTS

Preface   *vii*

Acknowledgments   *xvii*

Part One   Good Enough Is No Longer Enough

1   Changing Rules for Business Success   3

2   Principles of World-Class Execution   31

Part Two   World-Class Execution

3   Learning to Win in China's Many Markets   47

4   Developing Competitive Products   67

5   The Next Advantage for Manufacturing   89

6   Getting More from Sourcing More in China   105

7   Distribution: Changing Times   125

8   Talent Holds the Key   143

9   Where to Start   159

Part Three   The Future of Business in China

10   The Looming Wave of Mergers and
      Acquisitions   171

11   Win in China—or Lose Everywhere   193

Notes   *199*

Index   *203*

About the Authors   *211*

PREFACE

For those of us living and working in China today, perhaps no comment is heard more often from visiting American, European, and Japanese executives than this: "I'm amazed at how much China has changed since my last visit here five (or ten) years ago." They marvel at the dramatic growth in consumerism, most obviously seen in the profusion of restaurants and gleaming new stores offering a broad array of global and local brands. They express admiration regarding the boom in construction, the improvements made in infrastructure, and the enormous investments China is making in its future—such as the US$4.2 billion spent on a high-tech train system to ferry passengers from Beijing to Tibet. They note the increased signs of wealth and the willingness of government officials to relax the rules governing foreign-owned businesses. They are dazzled by the whirl of change, transformation, and novelty found everywhere in the country. Indeed, even those of us who live here are frequently awestruck by the historic events unfolding all around us. China is the story of the twenty-first century: an immense nation changing at an unprecedented pace.

But the pace of change in China poses a significant threat to the businesses these executives lead. Nearly a quarter million foreign (that is, non-Chinese) companies of all sizes operate in China today. Tens of thousands of these companies are multinational organizations (including 460 of the *Fortune* 500 giants) with business operations in China and corporate offices in Western nations, Japan, the Middle East, Latin America, eastern Europe, and elsewhere in Asia. Many multinational companies (MNCs) are thriving here, with annual double-digit revenue growth rates and plump margins. But these sunny days won't last, and MNC executives who work in China know it. The pace and intensity of competition between (and among) "foreign" and "domestic" rivals is accelerating quickly. Even as markets are becoming bigger and more attractive here—in some categories, already the largest in the world—they are also becoming more treacherous.

This book is primarily for MNC executives in the home office and in the region. Multinational companies urgently need to improve performance in nearly every aspect of their operations in China if they are to continue to be profitable here—indeed, if they are to survive here. Until now, many MNCs did not need to focus as relentlessly on executing to world-class standards in their China operations as they did in other markets. China wasn't like other markets. For years, winning in China (in fact, *being allowed into* China) was intertwined with securing government permission to enter the market, picking the right joint venture partner, and then selling existing brands at premium prices in the right cities to the right customers. It was about developing strategies for creating privileged access, and those who made smarter choices about partners, brands, cities, and distribution networks tended to fare better than rivals. Companies could always stumble in how they executed strategies, and in China, as elsewhere, bad execution of a good strategy has had dire consequences. But superb execution—on the level that MNCs would expect of their operating managers in competitive developed markets—was hard to achieve here, even hard to define. Multinational managers in China encountered a market that seemed to play by rules very different from what they found elsewhere in the world. As a result, they frequently tailored processes and practices to this very different world to get the job done. Also, they did not hold themselves to the same operating standards their organizations demanded in developed markets (such as manufacturing and sourcing measures, product development cycle times, marketing return on investment, and so on). For many years, that worked. Good enough was good enough.

That era is over. Today, China is open for business. Strategies based on creating and sustaining privileged access to a local market where global standards and measures do not apply look increasingly outdated. Joint venture partners and acquisition targets are available to the highest (or at least most suitable) bidder. Business licenses are readily available today, which was not true ten to twenty years ago. Rules are changing, and the landscape for business here is beginning to look familiar. Though China is still unique in many aspects—and probably always will be— today, China's fast-moving markets for information, people, and technology do not differ in their essential competitiveness from what managers see elsewhere in the world. Multinational companies, many of which are now expanding from their initial positions here, are fighting each other for Chinese customers and are increasingly competing as well with fast-rising domestic competitors that frequently possess better knowledge of Chinese markets and a dogged ability to operate at lower cost. This transition to a much more competitive and complex business landscape is dramatically ratcheting up the pressure on companies to find ways to operate at a comparatively better level of performance than rivals.

In other words, China is turning the corner from an emerging market, where local context drives most of the strategic and operating decisions managers make, to a maturing one, where top-quality execution is a cornerstone for success. Many of the bespoke systems and processes that MNCs put into place a decade ago now undermine their performance—and anyway, since many of the rules of business have changed in China, many old operating assumptions are outdated. Good strategy still counts, of course. But in a market where competition is white hot and global, the ability of companies to execute sound strategies extraordinarily well—across every operating function and core process of the company—is key to getting to the front and staying there. Suddenly, good enough is no longer good enough.

Multinational companies are at the very eye of this storm, which is why we've addressed this book primarily to MNC executives. Good execution in China is about adapting—sometimes a little, sometimes a lot—world-class operating standards, management tools, and frameworks to the realities of the Chinese environment. The advantage that MNCs operating in China have over their domestic Chinese rivals is their knowledge of, and experience with, such operating standards. Indeed, top-performing MNCs are frequently the very definition of world-class execution—*outside* China. But MNCs will only realize the benefits of their knowledge and experience if they can learn to select the right standards, tools, and frameworks from their global arsenal to put into place in China, adapted in the right way to optimize them for the local context. To succeed in China's evolving and increasingly more competitive markets, executives in China, and their colleagues and bosses in other countries, will have to change their managerial focus 180 degrees. They will have to put behind them tendencies to view business conditions here as simply unique, requiring in turn unique operating approaches and performance standards, and instead will have to focus on the familiar, seeing opportunities to instill practices and processes that are hallmarks in other competitive markets, tuning them locally as needed, and linking them globally at every opportunity. In the decade ahead, it is inevitable that innovations in management practice will emerge in China's hypercompetitive markets; MNCs that are prepared to spot these and move them quickly into their worldwide operations will be tomorrow's winners, globally.

A number of MNCs in China have begun to transform their organizations, to raise the bar on execution in order to win in China's burgeoning consumer and business-to-business markets. This book is about how these leading companies are succeeding and how other companies can, too. Although we highlight many best practices in marketing, product development, manufacturing, sourcing, distribution, and talent management in China today, this book is largely focused on helping managers learn how to think through the needed shift in emphasis from good enough to world-class execution in China, how to understand the principles of execution in this environment, and how to overcome challenges to adapting world-class operating standards to a Chinese context in order to be successful here.

This book should provide insights for a range of other readers, too. The principles of good execution in China apply to small businesses as well as large. The heads of small foreign (particularly Western) businesses in China face many of the same marketing, sourcing, and distribution challenges that Procter & Gamble (P&G), Yum!, IBM, and Motorola face. Although many of the practices highlighted in this book will not make sense for small businesses—hybrid distribution networks, for instance, or organizational designs for research and development units—understanding the path to success for larger companies may provide small business executives with food for thought as suppliers, partners, or competitors to larger businesses.

Finally, it goes without saying that executives of Chinese businesses also are learning to adopt top-quality standards for execution. Companies such as Baosteel, Huawei, and Ping An are investing significant management attention and cash toward understanding global operating standards and performance management approaches. We do not directly address their very different challenges and advantages in these pages. We would write a very different book for them: the strategic and operational challenges they face are frequently different in kind or degree from what MNCs in China face, and their organizational learning curve is also quite different. But the core message of this book—the way to outstanding execution in a Chinese context—is the same for both audiences. So are the stakes of the game. For that reason, executives in many Chinese companies will want to understand what their foreign rivals are up to. We have no doubt that if we were writing this book ten or twenty years from now—when we expect that a number of Chinese companies will be in the *Fortune* 500, and perhaps a few will even be truly global as well—the differences between these two audiences would be much less pronounced.

The old saying "The more things change, the more they stay the same" certainly does not apply when it comes to doing business in China. Each of the authors has been in China for roughly twenty years; today one of us lives in Shanghai, the other in Beijing. Both of us speak Chinese, allowing us to get inside the market we have sought to understand.

As partners in McKinsey & Company's Greater China Office—Jonathan has been with the firm twenty-two years and Jimmy fourteen—we have been at the very center of the changes we describe in this book. The insights in these pages reflect lessons learned in our work for over two decades on strategic, operational, and general management issues with MNCs in China, large Chinese companies that are entering the world stage, and parts of the Chinese government. We have been in the factories and boardrooms (in China and globally) of companies that are setting new standards for operating performance in China, and in factories and boardrooms of companies that, sadly, are not.

But this book does not just reflect the two authors' direct experience with business transformation in China. The firm of which we are a part has made substantial investments in understanding how to serve clients here, including establishing centers in China to study consumers and consumer behaviors and best practices in operations in China. We and our colleagues in the Greater China Office have conducted a number of research initiatives and developed several proprietary databases that we have drawn on for this book. A partial list includes the following:

- In-depth interviews with six thousand individuals in households in over thirty cities throughout China, from the largest cities to semirural communities. McKinsey's China Consumer Center is compiling and analyzing data from the market to understand what drives Chinese consumers and how they compare with shoppers in other countries. Our survey coverage currently accounts for about 90 percent of China's gross domestic product (GDP), 80 percent of its disposable income, and 60 percent of its population.

- A 2006 McKinsey Global Institute (MGI) study of urban consumers, including analyses of data from an extensive MGI database of consumption variables covering the years 1985 to 2005 in China, and econometric forecasting of future consumption patterns in China.

- A growing database of sourcing and supply management practices of MNCs operating in China, including in-depth case studies on supply operations at more than twenty companies (as of this writing) in a number of industries, and specific-issue surveys conducted with over fifty companies.

- In-depth interviews and surveys (conducted by the authors while writing this book) with the executives responsible for China-based operations at over forty MNCs in a variety

of sectors, including consumer products, energy, industrial products, retail, and high tech.

- Notes of in-depth conversations with the leading business executives in China conducted by ourselves or our colleagues (some of these have been published in abridged and edited forms in the *McKinsey Quarterly*).

- A study of the operations of ten large MNC research and development organizations in China.

- A study of talent management and performance management practices at three hundred global companies, and a comparison study of twenty-four multinational and Chinese companies using the same "performance ethic" benchmarks.

This book is the fruit of these and other research initiatives, of our work on the ground helping companies succeed here, and of our discussions with hundreds of multinational and Chinese company executives and owners or investors in many small foreign and domestic businesses here. It is also the fruit of discussions with—and insights and concepts from—our McKinsey colleagues in China and elsewhere, who are working with companies to help improve their performance in China. Their contributions were significant, and we acknowledge them later in this book.

Part I provides an overview of how the business landscape in China has changed within the last few years, and how it is continuing to evolve. The role of government relations—indeed, even how companies conduct government relations—isn't the same today as it was just five years ago. Similarly, the emergence of the global consumer has profound implications for execution, as does the war for talent. Chapter 1 shows how this changing landscape requires MNCs operating here to urgently apply more managerial attention to execution. Chapter 2 demonstrates just what execution means—that is, adapting selected tools and approaches, with an eye on certain key principles of execution that are specific to China.

Part II begins a series of deep dives to look at what top-flight execution means today in the core functions of a multinational company's operations here. Each of these chapters focuses on key activities to get right in China today and tomorrow. They describe the unique context for execution of these activities in China, and describe how companies operating here have boosted their performance in each activity by adapting to a Chinese context tools and approaches the organizations successfully use elsewhere in the world—what we call global standards.

We have largely organized these chapters functionally, beginning with marketing (chapter 3) and moving to product development (chapter 4), manufacturing (chapter 5), sourcing (chapter 6), distribution (chapter 7), and talent management (chapter 8). We've found in our discussions with multinational executives that this is the most straightforward way to organize and highlight what can otherwise seem to be a complex profusion of recommendations for change. This approach does not mean that every chapter will always address the full breadth of multinational readers, across a number of sectors, that we intend this book to serve—retailers don't manufacture, for instance—but most chapters will, and in any case, retail executives in China will want to see what P&G and other manufacturers are up to. Part II closes by providing advice on how companies can get started on making the changes required for them to raise the bar on execution. Chapter 9 introduces a framework for prioritizing and carrying through on change efforts.

Part III concludes the book by looking ahead at how the demands on MNCs' capabilities in China will evolve in two crucial ways in the years ahead. Chapter 10 looks at how the laws governing mergers and acquisitions (M&A) have begun to open up, and what this might mean for companies intent on buying growth in China. The flow of M&A shapes growth aspirations and industry structures everywhere else in the world, and we believe that in the decade ahead this will come to be true in China as well. Indeed, the M&A deal flow has already started to heat up here. Good execution has always determined whether a merger is a success or a failure, anywhere in the world. Companies large and small will need to understand M&A execution in a Chinese context to win at this game.

Multinational companies are bringing global standards and practices to China and adapting them to the tough realities of this market—to the cost constraints, the speed of market growth, the ambiguities and uncertainties, the fierce competition. Chapter 11 looks at how companies might use the adaptations they forge here to succeed in other emerging markets, and then in developed ones. At some point in the not-too-distant future, what is happening in China today will play a role in defining, and then redefining, the winning business model for nearly every industry. Companies that do not understand this and lead this change will be left far behind.

It's time for executives to move execution management from the back burner to the front in China. Too many MNCs have come here with visions of grandeur untethered to China's realities and are about to fail because they are not applying the same rigor to execution in China that they would in their home markets. This book is intended to help them succeed. To quote Deng Xiaoping, we must "seek truth from facts" and not let dogmas about "how things should be done" blind us to market realities.

ACKNOWLEDGMENTS

Of course, this book is far more the fruit of the accumulated experience of our firm McKinsey & Company and the people in it than it is the efforts of the two of us. Countless people have helped each of us separately and together over the years to develop the perspectives shared here.

While many of our colleagues made valuable contributions, a few helped us significantly to pull the book together. In particular, Paul Gao and Kevin Lane each contributed distinctive knowledge by leading the authorship of key chapters. Paul, who leads McKinsey's automotive practice in China, has a wealth of experience in distribution in China, both in automotive and in other industries. Chapter 7, "Distribution: Changing Times," is built around his thoughts, research, and insights on this topic. He is the real author of this chapter, which reflects the distinctive experience he has with local and international companies facing and overcoming distribution challenges in China. Similarly, chapter 3, "Learning to Win in China's Many Markets," owes everything to Kevin Lane. Kevin led our marketing practice in China and founded the McKinsey China Consumer Center. A fluent Mandarin speaker, Kevin has deep and unique insights into the realities of marketing to consumers and businesses in China. We are deeply grateful for the time and energy that both Paul and Kevin put into writing initial drafts of these chapters and collaborating with us as we collectively shaped the book.

We also would like to thank Ruby Chen, a consultant in our organization practice, who worked closely with us on the talent management chapter, and Chris Ip who, as leader of our Business Technology practice in China, was a frequent sounding board on IT issues in all chapters. Bill Hoover and John Stuckey helped us to develop an overarching perspective for the book and provided insights on how to make it a compelling and powerful contribution to the literature. Other significant contributors, including Thomas Luedi on M&A, Sasan Aminpour on manufacturing, and Gordon Orr and Yen Wang on technology, provided important insights that we have greatly benefited from.

We would also like to thank those who supported us in the process of writing. Michael Stewart and Stuart Flack provided invaluable stewardship, as did Lenny Mendonca and Andrew Grant. Josh Dowse gave support during the early stages to help us get our thinking and writing straight. We thank you, Josh, for the many hours you gave us. Paul A. Freiberger then moved the manuscript into something that started to resemble a book. Lily Jiang helped us to check many of the facts.

Most importantly, we have to thank Tom Kiely. Tom is one of the senior leaders of McKinsey's external communications staff and a member of the *McKinsey Quarterly* board of editors. He is not only a brilliant writer and editor but also a very engaged and insightful thought partner. Tom spent countless hours with us on the content of the manuscript, came to China to be with us and to "touch and feel" the subject, led discussions with Harvard Business School Press, and helped to shape the book's final form. Truly if there is one person who is our greatest source of professional support, it is Tom. We could not have hoped for a more constructive, collaborative, and talented person to work with.

Melinda Merino, our editor at Harvard Business School Press, saw the potential in this book from the start and artfully provided the right balance of encouragement and candid feedback to inspire us through final drafts and reviews. Thank you, Melinda.

Acknowledgments

We are also grateful to Hollis Heimbouch, editorial director of Harvard Business School Press, for her willingness to help publish this book at an accelerated pace.

Finally we would like to recognize and thank the many talented and dedicated businesspeople, both Chinese and foreign, who have made China the success story that it is. Several generously gave their time and thinking through several discussions on operating at world-class standards in China. In particular, we would like to thank Peter Ma, chairman and CEO of Ping An Insurance Group; Zhao Zhouli, senior engineer and vice general manager at Baosteel; Ambassador Charlene Barshevsky; Lester Ross, comanaging partner of the Beijing office of Wilmer Cutler Pickering Hale and Dorr; Grace Chen, previously an IP specialist at WilmerHale; Diane Long, head of sourcing for adidas; Kim Chang, CEO of Fuji-Xerox China; Klaus Zimmer, managing director, SAP China; Jack Perkowski, CEO of ASIMCO Technologies; Bill Haag, vice president of international operations for Preformed Line Products (PLP); and Wu Yu, managing director of PLP China. Through meeting and working with these thoughtful executives and leaders—and many more than we can list here—we have learned much and enjoyed much, and hope we have contributed to China's economic opening to the world. These leaders are the real inspiration for this book.

Part One

Good Enough
Is No Longer
Enough

CHAPTER ONE

Changing Rules for
Business Success

Procter & Gamble (P&G) is the most successful foreign marketer in China as measured by market share, with leadership positions in most of the product categories in which the company competes. In 2004, China generated almost US$1.8 billion in sales for P&G, or about 3 percent of its total revenues. Currently, China is among P&G's largest markets in sales volume.

The global consumer products company entered China in 1988 through a joint venture with Li Ka-shing's company, Hutchison Whampoa. Li Ka-shing was, and is, the wealthiest individual in Hong Kong and owns much of the port of Hong Kong, important manufacturing businesses, the leading supermarket and drugstore chain in Hong Kong, and real estate. He is well connected in China and was able to help P&G establish a business quickly and effectively.

Initially P&G marketed premium-priced products to consumers in relatively wealthy coastal cities. Over the next decade, this would become the dominant strategy for hundreds of multinational companies (MNCs) entering China. Most MNCs formed joint ventures with well-connected domestic Chinese partners and began to sell a range of goods—from cars to cosmetics, hearing aids to handbags, skis to scarves—that were largely existing products they sold elsewhere in the world, packaged here as global brands and sold to well-to-do buyers in the bigger cities. Industrial companies selling raw materials, parts, equipment, and services to business customers followed a relatively similar path, in that imported goods made by MNCs tended to be higher-priced and bought either in situations where there was no substitute or where the Chinese company required higher-end equipment.

Following this approach, the world's businesses flooded China. The tens of thousands of MNCs on the ground in China today hail from a broad range of sectors, including product companies of nearly every stripe (for instance, almost every Western and Japanese automaker is in China), global retailers, logistic providers, pharmaceutical companies, makers of industrial goods, professional service firms, technology enterprises, and food and beverage chains (such as Starbucks). Even in the insurance sector, where China has (under agreement with the World Trade Organization) only recently, and very gradually, opened itself to foreign-based insurers—it only fully opened the door at the end of 2006—more than half of the *Fortune* 500 insurance carriers are here.

The nature and extent of multinational involvement in China ranges broadly, of course. Motorola, for instance, estimates that its total cumulative investment in China to date—including a holding company, three wholly owned enterprises, five joint ventures, sixteen research and development (R&D) facilities, and twenty-five branch offices—amounts to US$3.6 billion. Preformed Line Products, a US$200 million Cleveland-based manufacturer of cable line fixtures used by cable and telecommunications companies, is also in China, producing, in a single plant outside Beijing, products for both domestic customers and global ones. Samsung's investments in China—including more than twenty-five manufacturing companies—amount to approximately US$4.5 billion. Mittal Steel purchased a 37 percent joint equity stake in a state-owned steel company for US$330 million in 2004, Wal-Mart has sourcing and purchasing operations as well as stores in China, and Novartis has sales and marketing operations and R&D facilities there.

The good news for MNCs is that the business environment has been relatively benign. According to the American Chamber of Commerce in China's annual business climate survey in 2006, 74 percent of the member companies surveyed said they are producing products for Chinese markets, and 64 percent indicated they were profitable or very profitable, while another 32 percent said they were at breakeven or suffered only a small loss. Moreover, one of every three said their operations in China had higher margins than their organization's worldwide average, and another one of three reported margins on par with their organization's global average. (One-third of General Motors's global profits came from its China operations in 2005, for example.) Between 2004 and 2006, margins increased for 61 percent of the surveyed companies, and another 23 percent remained the same.

The bad news is that things are going to get a lot tougher for multinationals here. The rapid changes in China that have created a hospitable business climate for MNCs are also fast turning many consumer product and business-to-business markets in China into the most competitive ones on the planet. Chinese consumer markets, for instance, are both growing and changing at a bracing speed. The McKinsey Global Institute predicts that China's consumer economy will eclipse Germany's in size in less than ten years, and rival Japan's in less than twenty.[1]

Enormous forces are in play. The massive middle class that has started to emerge in China's cities, large and small, has a buying profile different from that of the segment of consumers to which MNCs have been selling during the last five years. At the same time, the number of companies—domestic and global—competing for share of wallet in nearly every consumer and business-to-business category is skyrocketing. A spirit of entrepreneurialism is abroad in China. Overcapacity haunts many sectors here, and consequently prices in some categories (such as select white goods) have been falling for some time. Most other product categories will follow. Costs for producing, marketing and selling, and distributing goods are rising, and management talent is already a scarce (and increasingly more expensive) commodity. Merger restrictions are relaxing, portending a wave of acquisitions that will only exacerbate competitiveness.

Procter & Gamble has been feeling the ground change underfoot for the last few years. By 2001, the company's initial strategy—build significant market share for select products in select cities by cutting deals that create privileged positions—was running out of gas. The company needed to expand its markets to continue to grow, and to fend off lower-cost competitors that were nibbling into its existing markets. These growth and profitability pressures began to push P&G into what consumer product managers in China describe as the mid-tier consumer segment. The company expanded to new customer segments not only in cities where P&G had an established presence but also in new cities and regions in China. However, this put the company in direct competition with regional and national Chinese enterprises that often had lower operating costs and a better understanding of the territory. In some product categories, for instance, P&G discovered that the cost differential between a product (such as laundry detergent) sold in global markets and one that Chinese consumers outside the big cities could afford is so wide that, as many executives in China say, managers couldn't just take a global product and make it cheaper by removing or replacing certain ingredients.

To compete in this new terrain, P&G realized that it needed top-flight capabilities to discern new customer needs and to develop, market, and distribute competitive products to these markets. During the last few years the company has stepped up its game in every one of these areas (as we will discuss in some detail in later chapters). Today, as you look at how P&G executes each of these functions in China, you will find that its operations frequently resemble what you might see in P&G operations anywhere else in the world. For instance, P&G now designs products in China from the outset to meet a target price point, controlling for the costs required to meet the price. This approach—called design to cost—is a state-of-the-art practice followed in the world's top operating environments in developed markets. P&G has implemented the approach here to better compete in the new markets into which it is expanding. But the design-to-cost processes that you will find on the ground in P&G's operations here are also unlike what you will see elsewhere—it is design-to-cost with a twist. The twist is that P&G has modified the practice both to meet and *to take advantage of* the local realities in China.

Importing world-class management practices to get organizations in fighting shape for full-bore competition does not sound startling. But getting that done successfully in China—in a Chinese context—is a challenge. P&G has put in the effort and today out-executes rivals, both domestic and foreign, along almost every business dimension. A company that started out in the big cities of the east is today selling products in about two thousand Chinese cities and eleven thousand towns (and bought out its partner in 2004). Many other MNCs here are beginning to get into shape in the same way.

It isn't that execution hasn't mattered to multinational executives here in China. But for many years, companies thought of execution in China as something fairly basic and certainly China-specific, with little relevance to global operating standards, recognized best practices, or top-level capabilities. Moreover, figuring out just what constitutes good execution has seemed something of a puzzle here. How do you do any real market research (much less top-quality research) when half the tools in your global marketing toolbox won't work in China—and consumer segments are moving targets anyway? How do you design to cost when your manufacturing strategy was built on taking advantage of China's low-cost labor, not on eliminating waste and hitting high-reliability targets? How do you work with suppliers whose quality processes are widely variable and who cannot reliably ship to your factory on time? How do you brand in a nation where channels and behaviors, desires and images, are very different from those in mature, developed markets? How do you keep your product on retail shelves in far-flung cities? And how do you find and train talented managers to execute in ways that are at once similar to but different from how you might execute elsewhere—and then retain those valuable people?

It is no wonder that multinational managers in China have tended to create unique processes and systems on the fly. They have been creating manufacturing processes, for instance, to get products out the door in a reasonable time frame, at reasonable cost, by working around all the uncertainties involved in operating in China. They have been sorting through confusing, incomplete market data to try to understand customers as best they can. They have been distributing goods through networks governed by regulations surviving from an earlier era and burdened with logistics infrastructure challenges that are unimaginable to operating managers in the developed world. And because their organizations were founded on market-entry strategies that gave them a lot of breathing room (e.g., competition held at bay, influential partners, pricing power, affluent buyers hungry for global brands), systems, processes, and functions that basically got the job done were frequently good enough to live with.

That no longer works in China. In highly competitive markets, good execution matters—a lot. As we will argue throughout this book, companies intent on improving how they execute in China need not be daunted by the differences they find in the business landscape here (versus what the landscape looks like in more developed markets). And they certainly should not continue to create or maintain unique processes and practices for what they perceive to be unique terrain. Companies that are winning here have figured out—as P&G has—how to take top-quality processes and practices that work in their operations elsewhere in the world and adapt them to the situation they find in China. And they are prepared to adapt again because the landscape in China is evolving rapidly, and practice needs to change with it.

Strategies need to change, too—but this book isn't about strategy per se. We believe that execution, today and tomorrow, will play a much bigger role than it previously has in determining the relative and absolute success of companies in China. Executives will still need to answer strategic questions about products and joint venture partners, but they will also need to ensure—far more than they concerned themselves with in the past—that their organizations are marketing, producing, and channeling goods to customers at as close to a world-class standard as possible, despite—and in fact adapted to—conditions in China.

Our mission in this book is to help readers understand how and why good execution matters, and how to achieve it. Whether your company is one of the many that are leveraging China as a base of sourcing and manufacturing (and "winning" is about hitting targets for cost reduction and stability of quality) or you are battling it out with your international and local Chinese competitors for share in the domestic Chinese market, "getting things done" in China is increasingly a world-class challenge and opportunity.

A Look in the Rearview Mirror

It never hurts to look back to see where we have come from to remind us where we are. To better understand why and how the bar for good execution has been elevated, consider the experiences of the restaurant chains KFC and Pizza Hut over the last twenty years. When KFC and Pizza Hut came to China (both chains were then owned by Pepsi, but are now part of Yum! Brands Inc.), there was no quick service restaurant (QSR) industry here. There was no supply chain configured to move food through a QSR business, and barely a concentration of suppliers with which to forge a supply chain. Local governments controlled the retail sector, and joint ventures were the only way in. Even logistics were challenging: China was then a country with scarcely a provincial, let alone a national, highway system. But in those days just showing up truly was a strategy, and KFC became the first QSR in China when it opened its Tiananmen Square branch in May 1987. Pizza Hut followed in 1990.

During the 1990s, the restaurant chains started to expand their presence as economic reform policies in China changed and allowed them more latitude to grow. However, they had to compete with established local restaurants on prices and consumer preferences, and had to learn how to adapt. From the start of their expansion, the companies' executives realized that the brand in China had to be one that spoke to local consumer needs. The restaurants could not succeed outside the big cities if the brand remained largely a familiar American one with a few Chinese preferences thrown in for good measure. As the company learned, when it comes to food, Chinese consumers trust local brands more than foreign ones. To appeal to consumers here, KFC and Pizza Hut had to learn how to become rooted in China and integrated into the people's daily lives.

It was all about learning and execution. To build a local brand, KFC introduced children's programs to appeal to families (including creating a local mascot named Chicky), staffed each store with dedicated hostesses who welcomed diners and reinforced the local nature of the business, and created a real track record of community service. The menu evolved to appeal to Chinese tastes, with a few meaningful core products in each category, balanced across categories, meals, and occasions. A typical KFC China menu today includes items one would find in a KFC restaurant in the United States, such as original recipe chicken and twisters (for the novelty), and items unique to China such as oven roasted wings, breakfast twisters, winter soup, and seasonal vegetables (so as not to be *too* novel).

KFC also had to learn how to build an operating capability in China to compete with domestic rivals, and set out to be exceptional at selecting the best possible sites for restaurants, without compromise. The restaurant and its competitors both drew from the same low-cost labor pool, so that was not an advantage. To differentiate itself from the pack, KFC invested in developing outstanding customer service practices, beefing up staffing (which it could do given the low labor costs), and building a culture (today called the Yum! Customer Mania culture), that took customer service further. Training was a big part of culture building.

The restaurant group also built a logistics capability to enable its rapid growth, with a fleet of trucks and a number of warehouses across the country. And it invested in management talent ahead of the growth curve. Yum! now has the largest retail development capability in China and makes a US$90 million commitment annually to general and administrative expenses—more when factoring in its partners.

Today Yum! is the leader in both QSR and casual dining in China. KFC restaurants are located in over 380 Chinese cities—not just the handful of big seacoast cities that many other MNCs call safe havens. Because Yum! has focused on improving its marketing and operating capabilities in China, KFC and Pizza Hut are getting returns in smaller towns that are comparable to those the company is getting in the big cities. And the company's lead is widening. As of this writing, KFC has 1,695 outlets in mainland China, double the number it had just three years earlier. There are 260 Pizza Huts in China, too, with an average unit value of US$1.2 million, and sales growing at 20 percent a year. (The average unit value of a KFC outlet today is US$1.1 million.) By contrast, an MNC competitor increased the number of its outlets from 565 to 775 over the same three years.

But there are differences in how Yum! has structured its operations in China versus elsewhere. The vast majority of Yum!'s units in China are equity owned; less than 5 percent of them are franchises. This is a much higher ratio of direct ownership than elsewhere in the world. Why? Control is one issue. Yum! actively cannibalizes 20 percent of its store base so that it doesn't run into operational issues resulting in poor customer experiences. The company feels that franchisees would be less apt to cannibalize their stores. Second, the return on investment of direct-owned outlets is quite good, because the cost of building and equipment is very low (about US$450,000 per unit), sales volumes are about US$1 million a year, and cash margins run in excess of 30 percent. Finally, the banking system in China doesn't make loans on future cash flow. This may soon change, but given the returns, Yum! is happy to own the units at present.

Pizza Hut has begun to test home delivery in select areas. Eventually Pizza Hut hopes to offer one nationwide phone number for ordering from a full dinner menu, with expert call-center staff handling the inbound orders and neat and clean delivery services located across China. The company is offering the service to meet the needs of customer segments that are living ever more busy lives. Pizza Hut hopes to build the brand into the dominant "home meal solution" provider.

Today Yum! is opening over four hundred restaurants every year in China, and aiming for twenty-two thousand outlets in just a few years—a very ambitious target. Operating profit grew at 22 percent annually from 2002 to 2005, to stand at US$290 million in 2006. All of this was built on setting high aspirations, getting out of the big cities to target broader markets in China with new products and concepts, taking practices and processes that work for the company elsewhere in the world and adapting them to the China context, experimenting and learning, and executing well on all the core operating capabilities that count, including (for Yum!) logistics, talent acquisition and training, and store operations.

Yum!'s experiences in China aren't unique. The difference between good execution and world-class execution translates into significantly greater sales and profits, as we have discovered in company after company operating in China today. If the pace of change that we have witnessed during the last five years continues over the next five, the financial stakes will be even higher. The time to begin to improve execution is now. Companies that are lackluster at execution in China in 2010 may not have the option of beginning to turn themselves around at that point.

We believe global companies that cannot succeed in China will cease to be global companies at all. The size of the Chinese market, its increasing interlinkages with the rest of the world, and its transformation into the most competitive arena on the planet all mean that what works in China will increasingly become the standard for what works in the rest of the world.

Products developed and manufactured in China at low cost for highly price-sensitive Chinese buyers are starting to make their way to global shelves—including household cleaning products, power tools, and white goods. New technologies and processes are starting to emerge here that could ripple through sectors globally. For instance, one Chinese company has figured out how to get nickel for steelmaking out of slag that has extremely low nickel content; this could affect prices of the commodity worldwide in upcoming years. A Chinese pharmaceutical company is making an antibiotic using a Russian technology that is only feasible to use in China because it requires special machinery that cannot be made cost-effectively anywhere other than in China's low-cost labor environment. As Chinese companies such as microwave oven maker Galanz, white-goods champion Haier, and auto parts maker Wanxiang venture out on the world stage, they bring with them new business models based on having grooved their operations in China—new models that may prove to be a threat to MNCs in their home markets. (We look more closely at Galanz in the final chapter.)

Multinational companies will have to be in the trenches here, developing competitive products for demanding customers, seeing new technologies and processes emerge first-hand, and winning against new competitors in Chinese markets, to compete in global ones. The stakes are that high.

Evolution of a Management Practice

Another way to view the rising bar for execution in China is to look at the evolution of a core management practice for MNCs operating here: government relations. Even today, many MNCs treat government relations the way they always have—as bespoke, one-off, roll-of-the-dice moves led by "old China hands" on the management team. By contrast, a few top-performing MNCs in China have brought some rigor and discipline to the practice, treating it as a core operating activity in which consistency, process, and day-to-day maintenance matter. Significant changes in government's outlook on business and the economy during the last decade have helped drive this shift from treating government relations as an ad hoc "strategic" event to regarding it as a day-to-day operational capability.

As late as 1992, when Deng Xiaoping took his historic Southern Tour and declared "To get rich is glorious," business cohabited uneasily with government. Policies and approval processes for businesses were unclear, frequently driven by individual bureaucrats or offices with their own agendas. Personal relationships—informal, designed to give face, and occasionally laced with an element of personal enrichment—sometimes counted more than business issues. The Chinese landscape abounded with "guides" who stepped forward to help foreign businesses find their way in China, guides who claimed to have *guanxi*, or connections, that were frequently found to be tenuous or nonexistent. (Indeed, a singular weak point of this approach was that multinationals had to rely on fragile linkages—individuals inside or outside the company who professed to have connections—rather than systems and processes.) Typically the CEO was the focal point for relationship building, a strategy that worked best when the CEO had a passion for that particular task. In this context MNCs struggled to find a way forward that made economic sense.

Today the situation is quite different. China is putting in place a regulatory code not dissimilar to that in other market economies. In the last twenty-five years, China has passed more than one thousand laws and regulations related to commerce and distribution. The constitution now protects private property, and entrepreneurs are welcome to join the Communist Party. Constraints on foreign businesses have been relaxed. Whereas once the government required foreign-owned companies to form a joint venture with a Chinese partner to do business in China, today the government allows wholly owned foreign enterprises in most industries. This structure has rapidly become the MNC's approach of choice. Government also has established the necessary legal codes for mergers and acquisitions (M&A) of both state and private assets.

The roles of central and provincial governments in the business sphere have become more defined, and decisions more open and transparent. Central government, for instance, today tends to exert more control over industries earmarked for national development, such as high technology and aviation, but less control over industries such as consumer goods or food processing, where provincial and local governments—with their growing economic clout—compete to offer substantial investments to woo business opportunities. (The average city's GDP doubled during the first five years of the decade and is continuing to rise steadily. A province such as Shandong can negotiate on behalf of over 60 million increasingly wealthy inhabitants.) Multinational companies negotiate with Beijing, for instance, on deals involving multibillion-dollar gas plants and refineries. The national oil companies are critical business partners in these deals. Beijing retains the ability to block (but not necessarily to initiate) major investments regardless of industry.

As cities and provinces actively compete for foreign direct investments, they are fostering more and more rational and transparent behavior—a market effect, as it were. Foreign companies are actively driving this behavior shift by increasingly setting the rules of the game for new investments. For instance, companies will now frequently tell municipalities precisely what it is they have to demonstrate to win the proposed investment, and will stage multi-round auctions to extract the maximum in commitments from competing municipalities. These auction processes in turn prompt local governments to be much more transparent regarding what they are able to offer and (just as important) how they are going to interact with the foreign investor. Intel recently staged just such a process to finalize decisions on where to locate a flash memory plant it will build in China. Intel picked the western city of Chengdu for its investor-friendly approach, its willingness to help Intel access talent, and its clean environment.

The central government also leads significant efforts to root out corruption from top to bottom. In fact, in 2006 the government went so far as to depose the Party Secretary of Shanghai, the birthplace of China's Communist Party, on charges of financial mismanagement, along with many other leading officials nationwide. These remarkable developments mean that today MNCs in China will find a clear, well-trodden path for almost every activity they may want to pursue (with notable exceptions such as defense, media, and other still-regulated sectors). In this new world, personal relationships still matter but are no longer decisive. Foreign investment law is much better developed, arbitration courts are improving rapidly, and the government has even begun efforts to tackle the thorny issues of intellectual property theft in China.

This is not to say that China is beginning to be like the rest of the world in separating government from business. The Chinese government has historically seen the performance of the economy and of society as a whole as an extension of itself and its image. This is quite different from government's sense of its role in the United States or Europe, and even quite different from other statist societies in the world. In China, government continues to be an important determinant of the success of business aspirations. However, what MNCs need to focus on in their relations with the government to achieve success has changed.

In some ways this appears to be a dilemma. On the one hand, transactions occur, and the government is involved in every one (all foreign-invested enterprises need government approval); therefore, government relationships must be maintained. Moreover, the ability of a company to make future deals with the government rests on how well it executes the deals it has already made, including the service it delivers to customers and its ability to hit financial performance targets and thus return expected tax revenues to the government. It is critical, then, for companies to work with central and local government on a day-to-day basis to identify new opportunities. On the other hand, with more MNCs in the field, and much greater competition among foreign-based and domestic companies on the ground in every sector, government has almost no choice but to adopt more routine processes to manage access. The average CEO will find it much more difficult to see the minister in Beijing nowadays!

Multinational companies such as General Electric, Motorola, and IBM have taken this dilemma seriously and have ditched the old personal relationships approach to put into place operating models for managing government relations on a consistent and systematic basis. When there was more uncertainty and vagueness in government-business interactions, it was more difficult for either side to manage these relationships on a consistent and predictable basis. (Hence the importance companies placed on guanxi and individual relationships as a way to secure some stability.)

Successful companies focus on getting four things done very well. First, they systematically identify all the relevant stakeholders, at various levels of government, who may have a role to play (by influencing regulation or making decisions) in the company's various business areas in China. This can be quite complex, because there are many layers of government to consider and many different parties to, or influencers on, a decision. One MNC has gone so far as to identify not just all the current relationships it must maintain but also the next generation of leaders in China in all areas touching on the MNC's business; it is systematically building relationships with the latter as well.

After identifying individual leaders and government bodies, these companies understand in depth the agendas of each of these actors. Negotiations between Royal Dutch/Shell and ExxonMobil and Petrochine over a proposed four-thousand-kilometer pipeline broke down in 2004 after two years of talks when Petrochine's needs for capital and expertise shifted—and when a key senior official, whose final support was critical, remained unconvinced of the deal's benefits. That's a cautionary lesson no one wants to repeat.

After mapping out actors and agendas, best-practice MNCs in China take a good hard look at how they can adjust plans to align with these multiple agendas in order to create a balanced approach across parties. Finally, they develop systematic processes and clear organizational structures (with accountability baked in) to get all this done and to manage critical relationships on an ongoing basis—a capability for learning and for continuing to improve upon what has been built.

That's world-class execution.

Top Trends Driving the Need to Improve Execution

In every respect that counts in China today—customers, competition, costs, operations, infrastructure, and people—the bar is rising on how well companies execute to compete. To get a sense of just how important it will be for multinational companies to step up their operating game in China, let's look briefly at the key changes lying ahead in how MNCs develop, produce, market, and distribute goods and services in China, and how they play out as opportunities for those who can execute well here.

The Rise of the Chinese Consumer

With a half-trillion dollars in foreign investment on the table, multinational players are already present in virtually every consumer market in China. The affluent urban segment that most global companies targeted as part of their entry strategies turned out to be a large, receptive market. Today about 1 percent of the country's consumers are in this segment, earning over 100,000 renminbi (about US$12,500) a year.[2] Their buying power is considerable, accounting for nearly 10 percent of all disposable urban income in China (about 500 billion renminbi, or about US$62 billion), and they demonstrate an appetite for globally branded goods of all kinds. Best of all, this segment is largely concentrated in China's large coastal cities, so the costs to serve them are containable.

However, the pool of affluent buyers isn't growing nearly as fast as many MNCs had hoped. The McKinsey Global Institute and McKinsey's China Consumer Center estimate that the segment will grow to represent just 6 percent of all consumers by 2015. Moreover, although China's most affluent buyers, as a segment, tend to be loyal to brands, Chinese consumers as a whole are not. In surveys of thousands of Chinese consumers in multiple cities conducted by McKinsey during 2005, more than 80 percent of respondents said they would buy name brands occasionally, and nearly 70 percent said they favored buying global brands when they had the money to purchase them. But that does not mean they actually *will* buy an MNC product, even if they do have the money. We've found that price differences and point-of-sale strategies can sway a Chinese consumer's choices dramatically—in fact, as many as 65 percent of buyers say they frequently change their minds about what to buy once they are inside a store. And for all but the most affluent segment, there is a growing interest in Chinese brands.

The real buying power is shifting from the affluent to the middle class. More than three-fourths of all Chinese households today earn less than 25,000 renminbi, but within two decades that number could drop to just 10 percent. Chinese consumer markets may then rival Japan for the distinction of being the second-largest consumer economy (behind the United States), with annual spending rising to about 20 trillion renminbi. Upper-middle-class households (with incomes between 40,000 and 100,000 renminbi) account for less than 10 percent of all households today, but will more than double in size within the next ten years, and likely nearly triple in size again in the decade to follow, amounting to nearly 60 percent of the consumer economy. Companies that can serve this emerging middle class will grow faster than those that sell largely to premium buyers.

But here is the bad news: this giant emerging middle-class market is not yet definable. First, it isn't monolithic—we already see it fragmenting, as markets have elsewhere in the world. Second, the middle class isn't to be found just in the coastal cities, but also in second- and third-tier cities today, and even further into China's heartlands tomorrow. (China has an "urban" population of about 500 million, spread across about 660 cities whose socioeconomic levels vary immensely.) China's teens seem to be developing tastes and perspectives different from their parents, and well-educated young professionals are yet another recognizably different category of buyers. We estimate that outbound tourism will grow more than sixfold before the end of this decade, sparking global awareness and greater consumer sophistication among those who can travel and thus further fragmenting buying preferences and behaviors.

For MNCs, this means putting some real muscle into efforts to understand the markets that they will need to play in very soon, and then developing new products and domestic brands for these markets. Given how price sensitive these customers are, skills such as designing to cost and creative pricing will be critical. Costs will rise as MNCs reach out to customers in a broader swath of cities, and most other marketing and manufacturing costs are already rising across the board—managing these will be necessary for success. When companies could hang out their shingles in the big cities and sell to the affluent, there were fewer pressures to execute well. Now those pressures are mounting.

Competition and Costs

MNCs are already in a tough fight in nearly every category in which they compete in China. The sheer number of domestic rivals dwarfs the number of MNCs in the field. There are more than two hundred companies building cars and trucks, for example, and five thousand more companies making components for them. There are more than eight thousand paint companies, about five hundred of them selling more than US$1 million per year. There are thirty-three hundred Chinese pharmaceutical companies with substantial revenues (sixty-four of them earning over US$100 million), over one thousand consumer electronics companies, and over three hundred breweries.

As many MNCs have discovered, even if the local players initially ceded the high ground to MNCs, in the past few years many have emerged as serious competitors and are seeking to take it back. Sure, most local players are small and poorly run, in some cases protected by local governments. But they sustain market share of more than 90 percent in some low-end segments, where their low cost structure and deep distribution allows them to keep MNCs at bay. Local companies, especially large state-owned enterprises, have always led in the larger protected industries such as oil, telecommunications, and transport. In midsize industries as well, local competitors have shown impressive resilience to the MNC challenge by improving product quality, building brands, developing product and service innovations, leveraging their strong distribution capabilities, and, where possible, taking advantage of government support.

China today has large, well-run domestic companies competing in most categories. Among the most famous is Haier, a former state-owned enterprise that has become a publicly listed industry leader selling nearly US$13 billion a year of white goods and consumer electronics products. Haier has now taken that record of success overseas and aspires to build a global brand. Other consumer electronics players, including Galanz, Konka, and TCL, have also built large, profitable companies that cater successfully to, and have built substantial brand equity among, Chinese consumers. The same is true in other product categories, most of which now have established domestic competitors with a substantial share, especially in the mid and low price points, where MNCs have to date found it difficult to compete profitably.

As a result, where a multinational company might previously have captured market share by offering a quality product in a market that had not seen such quality before, now it is competing against both other MNCs and the low-cost and increasingly higher-quality domestic players. The competition is forcing overcapacity, now running at over 30 percent in many industries, including white goods, where, in consequence, prices have been dropping 5 to 10 percent a year for nearly the last decade. In fact, price wars are a common occurrence in many categories in China, and domestic rivals are particularly adept at gaining advantage through these price wars.[3] Although many Chinese companies are willing to accept paper-thin margins in these wars, it is affecting their profit growth. Haier, for example, saw a 25 percent profit decrease in 2005 despite soaring sales. Similarly, auto prices fell 7 percent or more in each of the three years to 2005, and profit margins fell from 9 to 4 percent between 2003 and 2005.

Prices are under pressure to fall, but costs are rising. Salaries are ratcheting higher, especially for talented people with the right skills and experience. Even average wages nearly tripled in the last decade. Office rental costs more than doubled in the period from 1995 to 2005, and in 2006 they climbed another 17 percent. We've seen the selling, general, and administrative costs of China operations mushroom at MNCs and domestic Chinese companies alike. Advertising continues to grow more expensive as demand for ad space outstrips supply. For instance, spending on advertising via TV, newspapers, and magazines rose from US$350 million in 1993 to US$18.6 billion in 2004. As companies begin to target buyers in the hundreds of second- and third-tier cities where the new Chinese middle class is now emerging, marketing and distribution costs will soar—as will R&D and product development costs.

The good news is that MNCs have decades of experience of managing under these conditions in other markets. The margins squeeze is a challenge that can be surmounted. The better news is that opportunities abound to reap big returns on improvement programs in China. A recent McKinsey survey of thirty electronics companies operating plants in China found that waste was so endemic in the factories' operations (compared with world-class plants run by some of these same companies elsewhere) that it reduced profits by 20 to 40 percent.[4] Making the effort to become world class at execution in China could pay off handsomely.

Business-to-Business Markets

Business-to-business (B2B) markets are likewise booming in China. Global industrial leaders such as General Electric, Hitachi, and Siemens all generate multiple billions of dollars from their markets in China in products ranging from nuclear generation equipment to locomotives. China has the most competitive environment in the world for heavy industrial projects, with competitive bidding on a global basis the norm at all levels.

Like their consumer product counterparts, industrial MNCs have treated China as an exciting growth market, particularly for established products with global scale and global technology. They saw the growth of China's economy as a great way to optimize their production lines while reserving the focus of their technology development and their base load of production for their more established markets. In many markets, China has surpassed MNC planners' expectations: China has rapidly become the world's largest market for power generation, coal mining, steelmaking, and many other heavy industrial products. (This has been a boon for Japan's economy, which has been sustained during the last five years by sales of capital goods to China.) This growth is driven by China's decided priority on investment-led economic development.

All this growth has created dramatic new challenges, however, with the greatest being local competition. Already producers of polyester fiber, textile machinery, and other relatively low-technology mechanical and electrical products have shifted production to China. Also, strong local Chinese competitors have emerged to challenge global players. The development of local competition has lowered margins globally in many categories as they, too, have begun to export goods to the world's buyers. The price of vitamin C, for example, has dropped by over 50 percent during the last few years, as has that of aluminum castings, automotive components, and many other products. Competition has also driven up the price of raw materials globally because China's industrial machine needs these fuels to compete. Iron ore prices are up 80 percent, nickel 120 percent, and coking coal over 180 percent above their levels in 2000. Oil, too, has risen to all-time highs, led in part by China's role (along with that of the United States) as the world's marginal source of demand.

Selling to China has become a much more challenging affair as well. In the beginning, the market was clearly identified as big state projects. (Baoshan Steel alone consumed almost 20 percent of the Eighth Five-Year Plan when it was first constructed in the 1980s.) With limited resources, the state focused its efforts on making sure it could get the best technology—and price was relatively no object. Now, as the market has expanded, the state of play has become much more price and market driven.

In fact, most of China's industrial customers today are not state but private businesses. Over 75 percent of industrial output comes from the nonstate sector. These entrepreneurs are in many cases small businesses, and as such behave more like consumers than typical B2B customers. In construction equipment, the average fleet size is three vehicles. This makes it imperative for MNCs to develop a much deeper and broader distribution network than they might in developed markets. It also requires more innovation in financing and marketing to reach and sustain relationships with a customer base that lacks the financial resources of a large customer.

Just as is the case in consumer products markets, so the days when an industrial MNC could simply go to Beijing and introduce its catalog and expect to win sales are over. Now it's all about executing at a world-class level—executing to compete against low-cost local competitors and to win the new private customers across China.

Distribution and Infrastructure

When MNCs first arrived in China, they faced a fragmented market, an inadequate infrastructure for moving goods or information, few wholesalers of any scale, and regulations governing how MNCs got goods to customers. Going direct, for instance, was illegal. As a result, most MNCs adopted multitier distribution models, essentially working through legacy arrangements established during the time when goods were scarce in the planned economy of the past. Multinational companies worked through layers of middlemen. Pyramids of intermediaries stood between companies and their end customers.

Today, the laws have changed and companies have more options for defining their distribution strategies—including going direct. Infrastructure has improved dramatically too. Many old China hands have nostalgic memories of moving product over potholed dirt roads to ports with limited capacity and outdated equipment. Now, complete and incomplete roads are snaking all over China. In the five years from 2000 to 2005, the Chinese added 322,500 miles of roads (taking the serviceable national road network to over 1 million miles), 4,225 miles of rail, and 402 deep-water port berths. A quarter of these new berths are on China's great west-to-east waterways, the Yangtze, Yellow, and Pearl rivers. Together, these represent a 38 percent increase for road resources, a 10 percent increase for rail at a time of a marked upgrade in the whole network, and a 74 percent increase for water.

The government has also invested in a twenty-first-century river for communications, funding the rollout of over 1.5 million kilometers of fiber optic cable during the years 1999 to 2004, effectively doubling the network to 2.75 million kilometers. The government's ambition is to have in place, by 2020, a broadband network roughly three times the size of the one currently in the United States. Here in China it is nicknamed the "800 Million Network" (*Ba Yi Wang*) after the number of users it will support. And China has been busy with more than adding power capacity. It adds more than 70 gigawatts of electricity generation capacity every year, a number larger than the entire installed capacity of South Korea.

Most MNCs, however, have yet to rethink their channel and distribution strategies to take advantage of these improvements. For some companies, old strategies are simply outdated. As they face greater pressure to serve customers in a wider number of cities, MNCs will have to squarely face the distribution knots in which they are tied up today and overhaul what are, in some instances, feudal channel structures. It's understandable that this is at the top of the execution agendas of executives in China today.

People

China's Confucianist heritage, rich in many ways, has instilled into the culture a tradition of hierarchy and respect for the innate authority of rulers, independent of performance. It hampers efforts to flatten organizational structures, or even to introduce team-based lean problem-solving techniques on the factory floor. The hierarchical mind-set is the product of three thousand years of bureaucracy and runs very deep. As a matter of course, state enterprises still promote employees based on rote learning of texts and in-job seniority. Although some assert that the state system or social conditions prevent bigger changes to personnel systems, the true barrier is typically the mind-set of senior management.

But we've also seen global human resources (HR) and talent management systems work extremely well in China. Multinationals such as P&G, Coca-Cola, and Johnson & Johnson have success-fully adapted, in their China operations, training methods that each organization uses elsewhere in the world. These methods include rotating talent through varied positions, both in China and globally, to expose them to diverse problems and management approaches.

In fact, despite the challenges, we believe good execution in HR and performance management capabilities really pays off in China, contrary to common wisdom. Why? We've watched as companies that put muscle into their people processes consistently attracted and retained the brightest upcoming managerial talent in China. In a country that is bursting with entrepreneurial spirit, China's young stars are attracted by global practices such as pay for performance, consequence-based management, training and development, and career programs—as long as they see it as a means to advance their careers.

China and its business environment are changing at warp speed. For multinational companies in China, the rapid evolution of markets and competition overwhelmingly demand an exacting focus (as they have not hitherto needed to do) on world-class execution. The next chapter highlights the principles that should guide the efforts MNCs make as they ratchet up their ability to execute in China.

CHAPTER TWO

Principles of World-Class Execution

When executives set about to improve how their organizations get things done—whether overhauling a function or broadly restructuring the enterprise—frequently the heart of the effort involves identifying and adapting management practices that have been proven to work elsewhere. Sometimes this is straightforward: dozens of companies have boosted performance by adopting the Six Sigma tools and principles that Motorola and GE pioneered. Sometimes adoption means adaptation: Alcoa developed its highly competitive production system based on the Toyota Production System. And sometimes the adaptation is more conceptual: in the late 1990s, the casino business Harrah's Entertainment dramatically boosted revenues and profits by building customer loyalty—essentially by adopting a same-store-sales-growth template borrowed from the retail sector.[1]

Best practices travel quickly in the developed world. We've all marveled at how fast process improvements introduced successfully at one company start to appear in rival companies within the sector, and then outside the sector as well. When Ford and others reengineered back-office processes at the beginning of the 1990s, it was big news; by the end of the decade new reengineering initiatives barely warranted mention in the press. Wal-Mart gained advantages during the 1980s and 1990s when it automated many retail activities that had traditionally been manual ones, such as tracking goods, and when it used technology to trade information with suppliers or to do more accurate forecasting. Now, most major retailers have followed the leader. Procurement practices developed in the 1980s are de rigueur at companies across sectors today; management development practices invented by GE and Shell are commonplace in the *Fortune* 500; and service businesses of all stripes are adapting improvement approaches from the manufacturing world, such as lean.

Adopting best practices *is* a best practice today. Good managers know how to spot them and how to get them deployed successfully within the culture and structures of their respective organizations. Over time, proven tools, frameworks, approaches, and practices, once unique to a handful of pioneers, become global standards. They become the obvious and necessary elements of good execution.

Recent research by McKinsey and the Centre for Economic Performance at the London School of Economics highlights just how important this process is. In a study of more than seven hundred midsize manufacturing companies in the United Kingdom, the United States, France, and Germany, researchers found a convincing link between how diligently and effectively companies adopt proven global best practices and company performance, as measured by such yardsticks as total factor productivity, market share, sales growth, and market valuation.[2] The researchers studied eighteen dimensions of management practice in three key categories: basic manufacturing operations (particularly shop-floor lean practices), goal setting and performance management, and talent management. They looked closely at implementation of practices in each company and graded how effective the practices were in moving the execution needle. Tracking production for a few weeks when output dips in order to wave numbers in front of employees' faces to spur action is a modest effort. Tracking performance indicators throughout production, consistently and reliably (not ad hoc), is better. But sharing information on daily performance targets in real time with shop-floor employees, assessing performance targets in daily shop-floor meetings, and assessing business goals in monthly meetings goes a long way toward managing for performance. It is the difference between good enough and excellent—and the research indicates it clearly counts in financial terms. (The researchers have since expanded the scope of the study to look at four thousand companies in twelve countries; the findings remain consistent.)

The link between world-class execution and top-of-tier company financial performance is so direct that it tends to overcome variances among countries due to local government regulations and market characteristics. Certainly there *are* country variances. Labor regulations in France and Germany are more restrictive than in the United States or the United Kingdom, influencing how companies manage employees in their operations in those four nations. Indeed, top manufacturing performers in France and Germany tend to focus on managing for excellence in shop-floor operations and on squeezing more out of the physical plant and equipment than do companies in the United States. In America, managers excel at setting performance targets and managing talent, and are less concerned with squeezing the physical plant because they can more easily turn to their workers for productivity gains than can competitors in Europe. Despite these variances, the researchers concluded that superior management techniques transcended all regional differences. Indeed, they found top-performing companies across all geographies, indicating that "how you operate is more important than where you operate."[3]

Top-quality execution counts everywhere—including China, or perhaps most especially in China. We've found that in MNCs that are executing at world-class levels in China, managers are doing what managers do best—adopting proven global practices, tools, and approaches to their China operations. A decade ago, it was not possible to transplant many standard business practices from the United States, Europe, or Japan, to China because regulations, limitations in the infrastructure, or cultural differences made inhospitable soil for these seedlings. But as described in the previous chapter, many of those barriers have fallen today, making it possible at last to adopt marketing, manufacturing, distribution, and talent management practices that successful global companies use elsewhere in the world.

But there is a critical difference—successful managers are *adapting*, not *adopting,* global practices. Companies cannot simply replicate in China practices used elsewhere in the world. Management practices, tools, and approaches require modification. Companies must tailor management practices and tools to accommodate the realities of China today. The differences between China and more mature markets can be small or large, and thus the tailoring required can be as little as shortening a cuff or as much as altering the entire look of a suit.

To give a sense of the range and nature of these alterations, consider the following two examples. First, because Chinese customers are "uneducated" (more so than customers elsewhere in the world), they frequently change their mind about purchasing decisions inside a store—switching at the last minute to another brand, for instance. Manufacturers have learned to deploy promotional staff to stores, even modern trade outlets, to ensure that their products are promoted effectively at the point of sale. The second example concerns a more significant adaptation: standard due diligence practices used by MNCs to assess business and operational information on a proposed target acquisition simply won't work in China. This is a country where companies often form without clear documentation of who owns what assets, and where records on mortgages and pledges are not kept systematically. Due diligence teams in China need new skills—and a different set of approaches and tools—to ferret out these sometimes murky ownership rights.

Getting things done in China thus requires global companies to carefully assess the admixture of global standards and local tailoring needed to be successful. The degree and nature of adaptation will vary by operational function or business activity. Based on our research on high-performing companies in China and our years of experience, it is clear to us that the MNCs that are and will be winners in China bring global expertise to this environment, leverage their international presence, and professionalize some of the valuable local practices they identify on the ground. But they also deal flexibly with local distributors, invest in extensive local market research, and uniquely segment their local markets. They develop dedicated personnel systems with stretch performance management targets geared to local realities. And, increasingly, they relocate key functions such as product engineering and global sourcing to China and use these functions to define new global standards in this new environment.

Four Principles for Execution

If getting things done in China, then, is about *selectively* adopting global standards, practices, and techniques and *adapting* them in a uniquely Chinese context, have we just introduced a black box? Are we arguing for bespoke execution? Not at all. Based on our experience working with winning companies in many sectors (including not only successful MNCs but also domestic Chinese companies that are beating their MNC rivals in some sectors), we find there is a set of common principles for executing well in China. These principles underlie all the tailoring and tweaking of global standards a company will need to do.

The next few chapters address specific global practices and tools that MNCs have adapted to advantage in China—why one practice was selected over another, how they were tailored and why, and what works or doesn't work—in six core areas of operations. But it is important to remember that the specific business choices and operating changes managers will make to improve how they execute should be informed by the following four principles, which can determine the success or failure of an MNC's operations.

Set Uncomfortably High Aspirations

Multinational companies are used to setting annual improvement targets for performance in developed markets. The company's executive team, for instance, might call for a 3 percent reduction in operating costs in one region or even across the board. The team might also expect their managers to boost revenues by 4 percent—or, aggressively, by 8 percent—in key established markets.

Executives should not settle for incremental improvements or modest targets in China. It is possible—and realistic—for MNCs to achieve annual cost reductions on their operations of around 15 percent and to expect to see the company's revenues rise by 30 percent annually. In fact, for several MNCs in China with which we are familiar, these should be minimum targets.

Whether it is revenue objectives or sourcing targets, net profit ratios or factory utilization goals, sales forecasts or delivery lead times, set targets that are far more aggressive than you would anywhere else in the world today. Good execution always starts by setting challenging but realistic aspirations, but in China, these aspirations should be big stretches because the opportunities are outsized—*and achievable*. Setting cost-reduction targets that are exciting but lower than what competitors achieve, or aggressive revenue targets that lag market growth, is a choice that could put companies out of business.

Make Readjustments Frequently and Quickly

How managers assess what works or doesn't work, the insights they draw from experience, the lessons they learn from failure, and their ability to reinvent as they go are critical success factors today. The more adept the organization is at learning and readjusting itself, the better it is at execution.

China, as we hope we've made clear by now, is a country and a business environment in rapid evolution: it isn't what it was, and it isn't what it will be. Ambiguity, uncertainty, and change are endemic to this kind of environment; learning and flexibility are necessary survival skills. Add to that the fact that good execution is the ability to take the right global standards and practices and tailor them correctly for this fluid environment, and you've upped the ante on learning and flexibility. Now add one more complicating factor: you won't have the cadre of experienced change agents and project managers that you have in your operations in the United States, Europe, and Japan. In China, finding a pool of managers who have good implementation skills forged by participation in successive reengineering programs is not possible—not in this decade, at any rate. Instead, MNCs in China are learning how to help managers adapt, learn, and grow.

For MNCs to be successful, learning will need to take place on another level, too. It is just as important for global executives in China (i.e., expatriates) to understand China as it is for Chinese executives in the MNC's China operations to understand the broader global corporate, industry, and competitive environment in which the company operates. As we've seen all too often over the decades and in multiple regions, when country and global executives aren't aligned—when they aren't sharing a single mind-set about what to do and why—mistrust and miscommunication sets in, execution slows down, and executives in both camps grow blind to market realities. Smart MNCs in China are already striving to bridge the divide, recognizing that there are differences in how the two sets of managers learn, reflecting educational, cultural, and motivational differences. These companies are helping both sets of managers understand that the objective is not to learn the Chinese way or the global way but to develop for their organization its own way to adapt global standards and practices so as to be effective in China.

Be Tighter on People and Looser on Controls

When adapting global standards and practices to improve execution in China, MNCs need to make realistic accommodations for the cultural power of hierarchy, local legal structures, and available skill levels. Hierarchy is so ingrained in the Chinese culture that if companies don't provide structures that mimic it, employees will create hierarchies of their own. Frequently, this can be counterproductive to good execution. For instance, shop-floor workers have been known to look up to the employee in their midst who has been there a few months longer than anyone else, even if the longer-tenured employee is *not* someone managers want to hold up as a role model. Similarly, salespeople in the field have been known to create their own little empires, building hierarchies rather than chasing revenues.

On the legal side, Chinese law provides unique rights to business entities, such as different assets on the ground in different locations—factories, sales outlets, and the like. This makes it more difficult to break up or restructure businesses in China from a centralized perspective; entities have rights. The talent shortage in China being what it is, executives cannot expect that skilled managers will run all of these entities.

Successful MNCs have learned to manage people much more tightly than they would in developed markets, and to relax controls to a degree they would not outside China. Whereas the management mantras in developed markets are to build flat organizations and let skilled and capable people run their own show, but to tightly manage controls and measures, good execution in China demands very different mantras. Here, you want to shape your own structure and hierarchy and manage your people tightly to help them develop skills they currently don't have, and you legally must relinquish some financial and organizational control to the local level.

The actions taken by the insurance company AIA (American International Assurance) provide an example. AIA built the most profitable insurance business in China by leveraging its experienced Hong Kong agency managers to recruit and train a small but highly skilled sales force that it then managed closely, applying conservative product and actuarial standards to focus on profit, not revenue. AIA salespeople have a stronger feeling of being a part of the company, and they view their jobs more favorably, than the sales force or agents of other companies in

China. The Communist Party itself provides another example of successful management through people. Its Organization Bureau keeps the Party unified by ensuring a consistent set of work experiences for cadres across the country, regularly rotating senior officials across geographies and functions every few years.

Measure Learning as Much as Results

In a world where change—particularly technology-enabled change—can be cataloged, codified, and copied, large companies can rely on tried-and-true maps for change (frequently developed by third parties, such as technology vendors, systems integrators, or process consultancies) even if they are planning change on a grand scale, such as merging an acquired company or installing an enterprise resource planning system. These sometimes massive 360-degree-change systems include process flow charts, ready-made designs for governance bodies and change organizations, checklists, milestones, time lines, measures and metrics, and best practices—all broken down in fine detail, and typically incorporating a sector-specific perspective (how to install a customer relationship management system in a bank, say, rather than in an industrial parts company).

However, these change systems rest on assumptions about people, existing processes, and infrastructure found in a developed market. Often, trying to match a change map developed in these markets to a function in need of change in China is like trying to drive from Boston to Chicago using a road map of the Ukraine. No doubt there will eventually be maps for systems or functional changes in China too, but for now most maps are at best approximate and provisional, or very general. Setting milestones for change programs and measures for performance is clearly as important in China as elsewhere, but it is more difficult for companies to do this in a systematic way than it is in developed markets. Frequently, just knowing what measures to rely on to mark the progress of a change initiative (and how to get the numbers) can be challenging. Sales-force effectiveness can be difficult to measure when distributors do most of the selling in rural markets far from an electronic infrastructure. Using Six Sigma tools to assess manufacturing quality is challenging when there are no established correlations between what can be literally thousands of input parameters and the quality of final product output. In these situations, management science needs to take a step back and deal with the reality of the skills and data available before committing to a massive measurement exercise.

In the interim, smart MNCs are paying as much attention to how their people are actually developing and learning as they are to assessing their performance, determining measures to use, and figuring out how to get the numbers for accurate measurement. This isn't to say that setting specific performance targets for individuals and departments isn't important in China—it is. But successful MNCs are balancing measures against the need to develop talent. Performance improves when the capabilities of employees improve. Firing a manager for failing to deliver on a business target—in a country where talent is scarce—may be, in some circumstances, a bigger error in execution than missing the target. Therefore, senior executives are both looking at other kinds of goals—people-oriented, skill-based, targeted, individual—and spending a significant amount of their time on mentoring, coaching, and providing in-person time with new staff. As an executive at one U.S. retailer told us: "We just have to get comfortable with the fact that our China management is going to have ten years less experience than management in North America."[4]

This approach requires a different mind-set from managers, one focused equally on learning and on performance assessment. Mentoring or coaching isn't a nice-to-have skill in China, it is the only way to escape the vicious circle of underperformance and resource reallocation. Leading MNCs realize this and proactively invest. At GE China, for instance, every new hire is assigned a buddy with one or two years' greater experience who helps the new recruit to learn the basics; later, the employee can select a mentor who will provide advice and coaching. GE China also pairs local talent identified as emerging future leaders with very senior managers, either domestically or overseas; such mentorship is usually used to supplement the succession plan.

Tomorrow's Best Practices

Finally, we believe that, over time, winning companies should leverage their success by globalizing their China operations. They must rethink China's role in worldwide strategy, organization, and operations, and integrate globally wherever possible. As China's markets intensify, philosophical distinctions are blurring between local companies and MNCs operating in China. Chinese firms recognize they must get onto the global stage before MNCs lock them in. MNCs appreciate the true ferocity of Chinese entrepreneurialism and hence the importance of beating (or buying) their local competition.

The most successful multinationals in China are successful because they are stellar at execution—specifically by "applying the global standard to China." But in the years ahead, that phrase may evolve to "developing the global standard in China." For many functions, what works well in China will more and more influence the global standard. Multinational companies of all sizes continue to come to China, and many of those already there are doubling their local investments, not only in manufacturing but also in sales, marketing, and product development. Some companies (particularly in high tech and consumer electronics) are starting to develop products first for China, then for world markets. China is fast becoming the center of world manufacturing and is not far from becoming one of the world's leading centers of engineering talent. With its increasingly talented, low-cost, and deep pool of technical skills, China may become a premium source of industrial talent and capabilities. And given that it is also one of the world's fastest-growing markets, and soon to be one of the largest markets, the intense level of competition may be setting a new bar for competitiveness that can be directed to other markets in the world.

In other words, it may soon be the case that companies have to win in China to win in the rest of the world. Given the scale of its markets, gaining a preferential share of a market in China will deliver a global structural advantage. More products developed in China will become global products; more practices and industrial processes will become global standards. The ability to develop a Chinese talent pool will be critical across all functions. Hence, as China merges into the global economy, we believe best practice in China will become best practice globally and vice versa. Astute execution in China will deliver a telling worldwide advantage, and it is not one companies can afford to concede.

These principles serve as general guidelines for managers as they adapt proven practices and approaches from their global organizations in their China operations. Part II goes into greater detail by breaking down this process by function, beginning with marketing in chapter 3.

Part Two

World-Class Execution

CHAPTER THREE

Learning to Win in China's Many Markets

For Jorgen Clausen, CEO of Danfoss, a global manufacturing company headquartered in Denmark, the realization came in 2004. He and his wife traveled the old Silk Road from Almaty, in Kazakhstan, to Urumqi, in China's western province of Xinjiang. As soon as he crossed into China, he noticed how the condition of the roads improved: the roadway was newly paved and modern, like a good stretch of road in Europe. Many of the buildings in this remote province of China were also new. A factory he visited was highly automated, and, at a department store in a fourth-tier city, the offerings included expensive dresses and $100 ties. "Something that particularly caught my eye was a refrigerator with inverters that control the speed of the motor and thus save energy," he recalled recently. "That was a luxury category one couldn't find even in a large Danish town."[1]

Clausen came away from his visit to Greater China with the nagging feeling that Danfoss wasn't doing enough here. Danfoss, which makes valves, compressors, motion control devices, and the like, had net sales of over US$3 billion in 2006, has factories in twenty countries, including China, and sells products in eighty countries. At the time Clausen was returning from his Silk Road journey, Danfoss was growing its business in China by around 35 percent a year, primarily by making (at the company's factory near Beijing) and selling European-designed components and devices to Chinese manufacturers. The nagging feeling he had was this: years earlier, Danfoss moved too slowly in markets such as the United States, Japan, and South Korea and lost market leadership to domestic rivals. His company's inverters were not in the refrigerator he saw in Xinjiang province. Was Danfoss once again losing out in markets that mattered?

At Clausen's instigation, the company launched a review of all its product markets in China. The conclusions shocked him. "We found that we were just skimming the surface," Clausen said. "We were capturing only a few percentage points' share in most of our product markets. Our products addressed the high end of the market and some of the middle, but not the low end, which in many cases we hadn't even known existed." The analysis opened his eyes to the shortcomings of the company's ventures in China. Although there was a growing pool of customers for Danfoss's global components, sales were constrained by the cost and functionality of products designed for markets other than China. One motor-speed control used in commercial refrigerators (engineered by Danfoss to meet European standards) was overengineered and too costly for many Chinese makers of commercial refrigerators. These companies were primarily interested in obtaining energy-saving functionality at the lowest possible price—and having it designed to better withstand dust, a need local to China but not to Europe.

"What stunned us was the size of the low-end market," Clausen continued. "We concluded that if we could offer the right products, there was a potential to increase our coverage by a factor of 10 and our profits by a factor of 30 in one segment of industrial-control devices—somewhat less in other segments, but still a very substantial amount. Collectively, this could give us a market share of from 15 to 20 percent, roughly equal to our share in Europe."

As Clausen noted, growing sales at rates even Silicon Valley chieftains would admire but losing market share was ultimately a ticket to nowhere. European or American companies that could not compete in broader Chinese markets like the one he visited in Xinjiang province—in the smaller cities, with lower-priced products, and with features appealing to Chinese buyers—could soon be eclipsed by companies that could, whether those companies were domestic or international rivals.

"We want to be a market share leader here," he said. "Maybe we cannot be number 1 in China, but maybe we can be number 2 or 3. We certainly don't want to become number 17, because then we will be in trouble later on when the industry consolidates here, and we don't have the volume to compete with local Chinese incumbents."

Under Clausen's leadership, Danfoss reset its aspirations in China. Today the company is aiming higher, much higher, and a sense of urgency drives his management staff's efforts. Danfoss now views China as its "second home market" after Europe. Clausen changed the metric the company focused on, from sales growth to market share. To pursue market leadership, Danfoss has begun to design products for broader, low-cost segments, has acquired other companies in China to expand its set of offerings, and is overhauling its R&D, manufacturing, marketing, sales, and distribution functions.

Danfoss is not the only multinational company in China that has begun to refocus its business. Procter & Gamble, Coca-Cola, Groupe Danone, Nokia, Samsung, and several other MNCs also have moved beyond their initial market bases—affluent customers in big eastern cities—and are selling to new segments of customers in a broader number of cities. Executives at several MNCs in China, and at many domestic Chinese companies as well, tell us that the game plan is clear to them. Becoming market leaders in the smaller cities will provide the scale needed to lower overall costs, allowing them to compete more aggressively even in their more established premium markets in China, and eventually even in their global ones. None of this will be possible if they fumble how they make these new markets and perform in them.

In China, as anywhere else, achieving world-class operating excellence is predicated upon having a clear understanding of the product mix needed to grow sales and profits. For companies in most industries in China today, the winning mix is changing rapidly. Clausen pushed Danfoss to reevaluate its initial product and market assumptions, and concluded that the portfolio needed to be changed if the company was to win. Other MNCs in China, particularly those selling consumer and high-tech products, have similarly reassessed their market strategies to think more broadly about their opportunities. Among the options they had to consider were the following:

- Continuing to grow sales of existing global products in China in their established affluent markets in the face of increased competition, price pressures, and rising marketing costs

- Expanding their existing brands beyond the dozen or more first- and second-tier cities in which they currently competed in order to reach a growing base of affluent customers in third- and fourth-tier cities, recognizing that distribution, marketing, and sales costs would rise and that they would face a new set of local domestic competitors

- Developing variations of their existing products and selling them at a lower price point, with some localized features, in hundreds of China's smaller (third- and fourth-tier) cities and rural areas, and even to cost-conscious customers in first- and second-tier cities, recognizing that the distribution channels would be different even in established markets (smaller retailers, for instance), as well as the marketing and communications channels

- Creating entirely new products in China to sell to existing and emerging segments, recognizing, as Danfoss has, that acquiring other companies in China is fast becoming one potential avenue for achieving this

A Continent, Not a Country

Typically, rethinking product portfolios and identifying market segments and products is a straightforward exercise. It's not an easy one—particularly in a world where products, segments, sales and service channels, and marketing and advertising approaches are exploding. Sorting through all the elements to consider, including pricing and brand strategies and setting the right investment agenda, can be challenging. But it's a challenge corporate and regional executives and their chief marketing officers at MNCs around the world know how to meet.

It is a challenge they face in China, too—with a twist. Here, executives must take into consideration an added layer of regional complexity. China isn't really a national market, like France or

Germany, Mexico, or the United States. In France, decisions regarding how to target a customer segment with a particular product—a computer game for men in their twenties, for example, or a shampoo for middle-aged women who color their hair—apply across cities, from Paris to Avignon, Strasbourg to Bordeaux. Marketing messages, sales channels, distribution costs, and a host of other factors differ depending on the *segment* and product you are trying to reach—young men, say, or middle-aged women—but marketing approaches and costs do not vary significantly by city.

In China, however, regional differences in products, marketing, and distribution costs count. There can be significant differences in the kinds of products that sell well in one region but not another, in the effectiveness of advertising or in-store marketing in one city versus another, or in the cost of getting products on retail shelves (and the kind of retail shelves) even for segments within cities. In a survey of over six thousand households across thirty cities in China, our colleagues in the McKinsey China Consumer Center found that buyers in third-tier cities more readily tend to stick to brands they know than buyers in first-tier cities do.[2] Households in the smaller cities were more receptive to taking on debt (commonly borrowing from family and friends) than households in first-tier cities. Most Chinese believe education is one of the most important investments a parent can make, but many more parents in third-tier cities voice assent with this attitude than you will find in first-tier cities. Advertising that is flashy or showy can be more effective in first-tier cities than in third- and fourth-tier cities; down-home messages work well with buyers in the hinterlands, but not as well with buyers in the eastern cities.

The appeal of particular products or product offerings differs regionally, too. Of course, this is true everywhere in the world, but marketers find that the differences can be more pronounced in China. Women in northern cities buy more color cosmetics than women in southern cites; in southern cities, women shoppers spend more on skin care products. Sea-flavored instant noodles sell better in coastal cities than in inland ones, where spicy flavors sell better. Taste-wise, China is a continent, not a country.

"Middle and western China is a much less mature market," observes Jean-Luc Chereau, president of Carrefour China, reflecting on differences he has seen between emerging and established regional markets. The global retail giant has been in China since 1995, and today, with seventy-three hypermarkets in twenty-nine cities, is the largest retailer in China. (China is Carrefour's fifth-largest market, growing at between 25 and 30 percent a year.) "Fifty percent of televisions offered in a store in Shanghai would be flat-screen TVs. When you go to middle China, it's only 20 percent because today flat screens are too advanced and too expensive for those areas."[3]

Important marketing and product differences exist even *among* third- and fourth-tier cities. For example, consumers in Haicheng, a third-tier city in northeastern China, are as driven to become rich as consumers in Shanghai or Beijing, and are stimulated by marketing messages that reflect this drive; they also place a lot of trust in foreign brands. However, consumers in Datong, another third-tier city in northern China, are far less motivated by wealth and are more skeptical of foreign brands.

Costs to serve vary among third- and fourth-tier cities, too. Distributors and large retailers, such as Carrefour, are found in some third- and fourth-tier cities but not others. A local government's experience with businesses and its receptivity to working with expanding MNCs can make the difference between success and failure in a smaller city. Among third- and fourth-tier cities, the degree to which the local economy is diversified or dependent on a single large state-owned business, local cultural differences, the quality of the local infrastructure, and other local factors can affect cost and profitability more than is the case in developed national markets. Thus, it can be profitable to target a customer segment with a product in one small city but not in another.

Marketers need to add the regional dimension to their thinking in China. The kind of trade-offs that executives must make when evaluating opportunities are more complex therefore—not product-by-segment choices, but product-by-segment-by-region. Can you profitably take existing global products sold to affluent customers in Shanghai, Hong Kong, and Beijing to underserved affluent customers in Yunnan and Nanchang? Are there opportunities to introduce lower-priced variant products in Harbin or in Kunming, where Carrefour has opened hypermarkets? Does it make sense to sell a high-end cosmetic product to affluent women in Yunnan but not in Urumqi, and a middle-market product in Kunming, but not (yet) in Harbin? Making market decisions by segment and product makes sense in well-established national markets, but ignoring the regional dimension in China leaves marketers flying half-blind.

Executives of MNCs did not face this level of complexity when setting market and product strategies for more circumscribed havens, namely, affluent customers in the big cities. Reaching out to customers in other cities and potentially other segments—concurrent with mushrooming competition and a rapidly evolving business landscape—raises the ante in marketing and in every other aspect of operations. But the process begins with figuring out the right product-market mix in this complex, fragmented, and continuously evolving environment. Once companies figure out who to serve with what, they need to develop new products with feature sets for customers who don't always know what they want, while under increasing pressure to keep the costs of products (and development) low to meet very competitive pricing targets. This is the subject of the next chapter. Subsequent chapters address how MNCs need to manufacture and distribute in a far more cost-effective and reliable manner to meet these challenges, and to recruit and develop the best people possible to achieve all this.

When companies stumble in how they develop a clear road map for defining who to serve and with what products, they create problems that ripple through every other functional area. Picking the wrong markets in which to compete will in turn drive companies to develop and manufacture products with the wrong features, make mistakes in their distribution strategy (and perhaps their sourcing strategy as well), and perhaps hire and develop some of the wrong people.

Companies that have taken a more systematic and thoughtful approach to marketing in this maelstrom of fragmentation have done much better. Those that have, such as Danfoss and P&G, have a clear lead in their efforts to expand to a broader number of cities, where the volumes are. In our experience, too many MNCs aren't doing enough at this critical first step—designing the right map for success—to better their odds of designing, making, and distributing competitive products to growing markets. They are not systematically thinking through product portfolios and segments, and aren't diligently factoring in regional differences. On the contrary, because growth has been so brisk in China, there is a tendency to jump on opportunities rather than to look across the portfolio and think about what markets the company must be in to win. For instance, we've found a few companies that simply took their global portfolio of products and fired them into local markets, hoping that something would stick. This fragmented these companies' spending on marketing and cost them credibility in the markets they were trying to enter. One such company, the division of a multinational pharmaceutical firm, spent five years taking this fruitless approach and never saw revenues for any of its products break more than US$2 million. Ultimately the division was folded into another subsidiary that was more successful. The subsidiary had taken a focused approach, thoughtfully picking products, segments, and regions and achieving market share leadership in its target markets. (It also developed a sales force to cross-sell its products in regions—a tactic examined more closely in chapter 7.)

Making the effort to look systematically across these three dimensions provides executives with a complete picture of what the company must accomplish to grow *profitably* in China, including changes the company may need to make in its sales force or distribution partnerships. The well-proven analytical frameworks that marketers use in their established markets, such as heat maps (multicell matrices) and the like, work just fine in China— as long, of course, as companies adapt these tools by adding the regional dimension to the mix.

Market Knowledge

A second unique problem marketers face in China is that market research is more art than science. If you are trying to assess how big the market is for your cosmetic product in Yunnan, Urumqi, or Harbin—say you've targeted women from households earning between 3,000 and 7,000 renminbi a month—you can't get reliable data. The government collects a great deal of public data, but it is fragmented across many different departments and difficult to identify, obtain, and—if necessary—pull together. The quality of the data and of measurement criteria also varies widely. As a result, it is hard to find information granular enough to make market decisions as confidently as you can in mature markets. With some effort, you may be able to identify the number of "high-income" households in certain cities, but the income range aggregated within that segment could range widely. Similarly, it is difficult to get granular information on family size, age distributions, employment, or other useful data filters to size market potential. Even if you could get that kind of data, demographic changes are occurring so rapidly and the pace of income growth is changing so quickly that what you're looking at is outdated even if it's supposedly "recent" numbers.

Eventually this information deficit will improve. Third-party data collectors and most of the major industry analysts are now operating in China, and it will only be a matter of time before they offer more reliable market information. The largest retailers in China have started to capture point-of-sale data. Although this pool of data, too, is shallow and can't provide the level of information manufacturers routinely get in mature markets, improvements will come year by year. Some local market analysts, each focused on a sector within their own regions, can provide useful information, particularly when the company's marketing team can carefully coach the research firm.

Information for marketers is thus incomplete today. Fortunately, however, it is relatively simple, straightforward, and inexpensive for MNC marketers to collect their own data. China has a large, talented pool of surveyors that can do large-scale research quickly and at a reasonable cost. One industrial products company recently completed a survey of over six hundred businesses—each survey lasting approximately one hour and comprising both a qualitative and quantitative aspect—in less than six weeks and for less than US$100,000. The data provided by the survey generated insights that helped the company's product developers make what turned out to be valuable decisions concerning features to include in a product the company successfully introduced, and helped the sales force to focus its messaging regarding the product.

Similarly, a high-tech company conducted one-hour interviews with the decision maker in four thousand households across urban China. Using well-trained college students and recent college graduates to conduct the survey, it took six weeks to complete the interviews and four weeks to analyze the findings, and cost just US$200,000. The findings helped shape the company's decisions about segments to target in a broad number of cities of different sizes. Additional research helped them to prioritize cities and to match products, segments, and regions.

Given the size of the opportunity that most companies have in China and the investments being made in hard assets and organization, investments in understanding market size, segment characteristics and behaviors, and product development insights are well worth the relatively modest (and variable) cost of hiring surveyors.

The Brand Challenge

A trend we have begun to see emerge in the last few years, but particularly during 2006 and early 2007, is an increased partiality by Chinese consumers for Chinese brands rather than foreign ones. In surveys conducted by McKinsey's China Consumer Center, the overall percentage of consumers across China who said they trust only Chinese brands rose to 53 percent in 2006, from 46 percent in 2005—a significant increase. Similarly, fewer consumers voiced strong or even moderate trust in foreign brands. Younger, more affluent males in first-tier cities seem to be strong partisans of foreign brands, but in every other customer segment, region, and age group, there is rising interest in domestic over foreign brands.[4]

There may be many reasons for this shift. First, the rising sense of confidence and pride the Chinese feel for China could be influencing a renewed desire by consumers to support Chinese enterprises. Chinese consumers, traditionally conservative, may be becoming more traditional in part as a reaction to change in general, and in particular to the dramatic increases in wealth and the changes in lifestyles that are under way. Second, foreign brands really haven't deeply penetrated markets outside the big cities; domestic brands hold sway in these markets. Finally, the media published a number of negative news stories about foreign brands during 2006 and gave increased voice to "buy Chinese" sentiments. Culturally, Chinese are inclined to be swayed by the opinions of authority figures, elders, and peers.

The growing preference for Chinese products is strong across most categories. But consumers seem to trust domestic brands most particularly in household care products, pharmaceuticals, household appliances, and beauty and hair care products. They are less strongly devoted to Chinese brands when it comes to automobiles and consumer electronics gear. But whether voicing a preference for domestic or foreign brands, consumers say their top reason for choosing one is quality (or superior product and performance)—across the board, in category after category. Chinese consumers are also more price sensitive than consumers in developed markets such as the United States, the United Kingdom, or Japan. They are less likely than consumers in those other markets to accept price premiums, and are very resistant to attempts to increase prices, even modestly, once prices are established.

It's worth noting that many Chinese consumers are confused about brands. During 2006, our colleagues in the China Consumer Center tested almost forty foreign brands in five categories—pharmaceuticals, diapers, toothpaste, beverages, and consumer electronics—with Chinese consumers in a variety of cities and segments. Nearly 70 percent of consumers believed that several beverages marketed by foreign companies were, in fact, domestic brands. Eighty-four percent thought that the product made by a foreign company among the tested pharmaceuticals was a Chinese brand. Numbers were similar among the diaper and toothpaste products tested. Consumers were pretty quick to identify consumer electronics products as foreign brands, however.[5]

Thus, one way MNCs can appeal to buyers in smaller cities and among the middle class is by being as "local" as possible. Novartis markets Voltaren, a pain medication, as a Chinese product. There is no English name on the product's packaging, or even an English word in an inconspicuous place (as is the case with many other Western products). Novartis ads show only the Chinese name of the company, which translates as "Chinese Promise." The product is endorsed by Chinese celebrities, such as the China National Gymnastics Team.

Rapidly introducing new products is another possible strategy. P&G has introduced lower-priced Crest toothpaste products to reach mass consumers in a wide number of cities. It has been building market leadership for Crest by continually introducing new products that build on aspects of Chinese customs, such as the use of extracts from salt, green tea, and jasmine. In the mobile handset market, Nokia is market leader in part because it can rapidly offer customers new products with advanced features, keeping domestic rivals that launch lower-cost knock-off products at bay and creating a sense among consumers of superior value, quality, and innovation.

The Learning Imperative

The foregoing discussion suggests that expanding into smaller tiers will be quite challenging for foreign companies. Companies will learn their way into markets where buyers are learning about consumerism. China's markets are not only widely variable and difficult to size and fathom, but also quite fluid and changing rapidly. Many brands, and even entire categories, have only been introduced to China in the past ten to twenty years, and many consumers achieved spending power for the first time during the same period. In a culture where people listen to authority figures and trust the opinions of peers, MNCs can establish new markets with the middle class by developing marketing approaches that educate consumers about products (or even whole categories) and in the process shape user expectations and impressions and build brand trust. Most critically, marketers themselves must be prepared to experiment with approaches, figure out what works (or doesn't) and why, and adapt, refine, and progress.

The point of sale, for instance, is rapidly becoming a classroom for buyers and sellers alike. We find that Chinese consumers are highly susceptible to point-of-sale pitches from product sales-people or in-store promotions. As mentioned in chapter 1, McKinsey studies indicate that when buyers enter a store intending to buy a certain brand of a product, 65 percent of them walk out the door with an entirely different brand in their arms.[6]

Given this behavior, smart manufacturers have learned to send promoters into hypermarkets and grocery stores to help educate buyers and ultimately influence the brands they buy. The promoters dress in store uniforms and help customers with product knowledge—they are like helpful and knowledgeable specialists who can talk a consumer though what the category is, how features work, how consumers use them, problems to look out for and how to solve them, and so on. Manufacturers also set up "shop in shop" displays, where they demonstrate products and answer questions, often with remarkable patience. As another example, auto dealers in China spend more time educating customers than dealers do anywhere else: a high percentage of the prospective buyers who walk through dealers' doors are first-time buyers, and even sales staff may never have owned a car.

The jury is still out on how to most effectively advertise in China, and companies will need to continue to experiment with ways to promote products through different media. The situation seems volatile, with Chinese consumers learning about advertising even as they learn about products and categories. Ten to fifteen years ago, Chinese consumers loved television ads—ads were interesting, novel. Advertisements on television and in the explosion of new magazines that have reached the newsstands since the early 1990s also provided Chinese consumers with glimpses of new ways to think about style and fashion, about how they decorated or maintained their homes, or how they ate. New studies, however, suggest that Chinese consumers are tuning out this bombardment of marketing messages.[7] They resist them even more fiercely than consumers in developed markets. For instance, in 1999, Chinese television viewers switched channels or left the room when ads appeared on the screen 42 percent of the time. By 2004, viewers were turning away from ads 72 percent of the time—that's more than viewers in most developed nations.

At least for now, P&G and other companies have concluded that television is a fundamental advertising medium in China, perhaps even more so than in some developed markets, because of its broad reach as compared with many other fragmented media vehicles. In McKinsey surveys with consumers, TV ads clearly still have a broader reach than newspaper ads, billboards, bus or radio ads, Internet and mobile short message service (SMS) marketing, and ads in cinemas or in elevators. Other media, such as print magazines, newspapers, and radio, are become more useful mechanisms for reaching consumers but remain well behind TV in penetration, especially outside the top cities. P&G advertises both on national television channels (such as CCTV) and city channels (such as those operated by the Shanghai Media Group), which P&G has found to be a very effective tactic in those regions.

The cost of advertising is going up, however. Take television, for instance. In the annual auction of TV spots held by the national broadcaster, CCTV, companies have been fighting to outbid each other for the spots with the greatest reach, with the total auction value growing to US$724 million in 2005. In 1995 Kongfu Spirit topped the spending with US$3.7 million, but in 2005 Procter & Gamble spent US$43 million, and a domestic dairy company, Yili, came in second at US$30.6 million, followed by another dairy company—Bright Dairy & Food Company—at US$27.7 million.

Moreover, we've found that a substantial number of consumers trust recommendations from friends and relatives when choosing certain household or beauty products. In fact, although television has broader reach, word of mouth has a deeper impact on consumers' buying decisions in China—unlike consumers in developed markets, who are much more independent in their buying considerations. This suggests that viral marketing—still in its infancy here—could become an important marketing tool in China, perhaps even more so than in developed markets. Similarly, sponsorships help create an aura of credibility around a brand—it is like getting a recommendation from a trusted source.

Another reason to experiment and learn: Chinese attitudes toward brands are complex and evolving. Face is important to Chinese consumers, and a significant number voice strong desires to own products with famous brands. (Indeed, among a minority of buyers who say they always buy famous brands, the desire to own brands is strongest for products that are typically visible to others around them, such as cars, mobile phones, and MP3 players.) But overall they are less brand loyal than buyers in developed markets—

except when shopping for select brands they prefer and that are in important categories for them, in which case they choose not to buy rather than switching to another brand. China's teens—the next generation of buyers—are exposed to a number of foreign brands, from Motorola phones to Nike shoes and KFC restaurants, and like teens everywhere are more brand conscious than their parents. They are also more trusting of foreign brands—65 percent of China's teenagers trust foreign brands. Additionally, young workers in their twenties and thirties have more disposable income than their parents do (unlike twenty-year-olds in developed nations) and seem to like to experiment with brands.

It is too soon to tell where all these trends are headed. The only thing one can say for certain is that things will change. Each year, twenty million Chinese teenagers turn eighteen. That is a cohort the size of Australia. Each year, there are fifteen million new urbanites peeking into store windows, and eight million newly married couples whose consumption patterns will change. China leads the world in soft-drink consumption, but average consumption per person in China is miniscule compared with most developed countries, suggesting significant room to grow. Sixteen million Chinese tourists visited cities and countries around the world last year, and we expect this number to grow to one hundred million in five years. The list of big and rapid changes in markets goes on and on, in category after category.

It is a fluid environment. Marketing in China is a game of soccer, not American football. In American football, teams carefully choreograph their plays. When a ball is snapped and a play works, it is poetry in motion, but when the play fails, the team finds itself back at the line of scrimmage, where it started. In soccer, the team knows which goal it is aiming for and has some basic plays worked out. However, the key to success in soccer lies in being flexible and situational, creating and taking advantage of opportunities in a constantly changing environment.

In particular, the environment favors a willingness to test new ideas, regularly and swiftly—new products, new packaging, new price points, and new marketing tactics. Some tests inevitably fail. (If you haven't failed recently in China, you haven't been taking enough risks.) In addition to trying new ideas, you have to try them quickly—not reacting to the "flavor of the month," but rather responding to clear market signals. Audi, for example, saw private luxury car buyers emerge in numbers in the late 1990s, and responded by building a network of quality dealer showrooms with innovative architectural designs full of comforts for their customers. Not only were the showrooms the first of their kind in China, but their design and efficiency were consistent with Audi's own brand positioning. The channel reinforced the brand.

Finally, markets and consumers learn, too, and companies would be wise—in some particularly quicksilver segments—to shape the early experiences of nascent markets. This is a unique opportunity. In China, where many categories are brand new to consumers and where buyers are curious and willing to explore, MNCs can leverage their brand-building experiences in other world markets to help Chinese consumers adopt something new. Starbucks, for instance, is investing aggressively in China, believing it could become one of Starbucks's biggest markets. China is not a coffee culture—it is a tea culture. But Starbucks is trying to create a coffee culture in this tabula rasa market by introducing Chinese consumers to the Starbucks *experience* and the beverages that come with it.

Today and tomorrow, marketers in China must be able to monitor changes in their product areas and adapt to them more quickly than in most other markets around the world, against fierce competition, and in an atmosphere of flux and uncertainty—and the absence of complete data. The best of them will proactively shape emerging markets and customer segments, leveraging marketing capabilities by learning and adapting quickly. The best of the best will take capabilities learned in China and apply them to marketing more aggressively in home markets. A crucial aspect of this process is developing competitive products, the topic of the next chapter.

CHAPTER FOUR

Developing Competitive Products

Understanding clearly the mix of products and segments (and regional differences among segments) that the company will address provides an overall game plan for expanding markets in China. Executing in top form the various marketing practices and capabilities needed to achieve this—performing product, segment, and region analyses; obtaining market information despite limitations; experimenting with and learning from marketing approaches through the mass media, personal and direct channels, and at the point of sale—ensures at least relative advantage in marketing muscle against rivals that are less systematic in approach or can't learn as well or as fast.

Marketers—along with researchers, engineers, and designers—also help their companies develop products to win in these markets.

Expanding a company's market footprint in China requires development of products that will appeal to less affluent Chinese consumers in less wealthy cities and regions, with features customers value and at prices they are willing to pay. But just as marketers cannot simply deploy world-class analytical approaches in China without adapting them to local realities, or count on having the same kind of information resources that they would have access to in developed markets, so too product development teams become world class in China by taking frameworks, processes, and approaches proven to be effective in developed markets and adapting them to the realities of China.

Let's begin our dive into product development in China by taking a look at a hit product: the Motorola A6288 mobile phone. Motorola opened its first sales office in Beijing in 1987, began manufacturing telecommunications products at its plant in Tianjin in 1992, and opened its first R&D center in Beijing in 1993. Today, Motorola has eighteen R&D centers in China, located in cities such as Shanghai, Suzhou, Guangzhou, Hong Kong, and Chengdu. The centers have a combined staff of more than eight hundred engineers and marketing professionals, research relationships with nineteen Chinese universities and research centers, and an annual budget exceeding US$200 million.

The A6288 was the first product developed by China's R&D staff, and was launched in 2001. In fact, this was the first product Motorola had ever developed outside the United States, and it was the first phone designed specifically for the Chinese market by a non-Chinese company. It took 148 engineers fourteen months to develop, and incorporated key local features such as—a first—Chinese handwriting recognition technology. The phone was a hit with Chinese buyers, allowing Motorola to take—provisionally—a leadership position in the market against global and domestic rivals, in a sector that had become fiercely competitive.

Research and development operations of this magnitude are something of an anomaly in China. With notable exceptions, such as P&G, most multinational companies in China have just begun to step up their product development efforts within the last few years. IBM has had a research center in China since 1995, and Microsoft since 1998, but DuPont's US$20 million research center in Shanghai just opened, as did Novartis's and Estée Lauder's centers. According to government figures, there were two hundred foreign-based R&D centers in China in 2000, but by 2005 that number had grown to seven hundred fifty.

As long as they could make markets for their existing global products in China, MNCs did not need to build and maintain the kind of top-flight product development capabilities they have in place elsewhere. On the contrary, MNCs have kept their product development investments in China more modest. In fact, for some MNCs this has meant little more than quartering small teams of development staff in manufacturing plants, where the teams have largely focused on prototyping, process engineering, and material specification work. Even for MNCs that have more robust development operations—with customer insight teams, branding professionals, and engineers—the capabilities are not at the level of performance many of these companies expect from their product development operations in other markets. Instead, they focus on making minor changes to existing products to meet local tastes.

But now those investments are growing, as are expectations for R&D productivity. In a 2006 McKinsey study of ten large multinational company R&D operations in China, we found that multinationals are stepping up investments for two reasons. First, of course, they are seeking to ramp up development of products for local markets and to better tailor global products to Chinese markets. But over the longer term, each of them is planning to expand broader R&D efforts in China, moving some activities conducted elsewhere in the world to China to reduce overall R&D expenses. They also want to tap local R&D talent, find local innovations they can take to broader regional (i.e., Asian) or global markets, and obtain access to Chinese research at universities, R&D centers, and Chinese entrepreneurial firms. Finally, companies that manufacture in China also want to move R&D there to reduce time to market.[1]

As the investments get bigger, the need to make the most of those investments also increases. That means getting R&D assets in China to perform at standards the company would expect anywhere in the world. As multinational companies compete against global and domestic rivals in what are for the MNCs frequently new and unknown markets, wooing customers whose preferences may differ from those of buyers in the big cities (differences that are sometimes subtle, sometimes not), at decidedly lower price points, nothing less than top-quality execution counts. In fact, it may count more in China than anywhere else. Already, some products from MNCs are winning in these new markets, such as toothpaste from Colgate-Palmolive containing Chinese traditional medicines. In other instances, markets are dominated by rival domestic companies that have introduced innovations buyers want. For instance, Chinese white-goods manufacturer Haier gained dominance in some rural markets in 2004 when it introduced a washing machine that doubled as a potato washer. (Farmers loved it.) In either case, the battle centers on good product development.

In more mature sectors in China, companies that get product development right are already starting to outperform companies that don't. Shanghai General Motors (SGM), for example, has a team of eight hundred engineers refining GM's Regal, Century, and Excelle designs for the local market, making more changes to the base model to suit local preferences than most other global automakers are. The China features include some styling elements, more controls that are accessible from the back seat (because a higher proportion of car owners in China have drivers than in the West), and a storage compartment for drying umbrellas. SGM cars also have air-filtering systems that can stand up to the higher pollution counts in China. (In addition, retractable side-view mirrors, which have become more common in cars sold in developed countries, first appeared on cars in China to make parking easier in tight parking spaces.) Partly as a result of such efforts, SGM has seen its market share more than double, from 4.9 percent in 2000 to 11.2 percent in 2005. Price also counts: Chevrolet Sparks, produced at another General Motors joint venture (with Wuling and Shanghai Automotive Industry Corporation), are selling for as low as US$6,200. The same joint venture also makes a vehicle selling under the Wuling local brand, with sales prices starting at US$3,500.

Good product development is necessary to hold onto existing markets in China. It is a ticket to play for any MNC that wants to succeed in emerging high-volume, middle-class markets. A number of multinational companies are betting that their product development operations in China eventually will become a hub for their global R&D efforts, particularly in categories where the heat of competition is, or will soon become, the most intense in the world, including many high-tech and consumer electronics areas.

What's the logic for that gamble? They estimate that making China a base for R&D could add up to significant savings, particularly in sectors where R&D is a large and growing portion of a product's cost base. High-end telecommunications routers constitute one of these markets. To understand the impact of moving R&D to China, we compared the router costs of an American and a Chinese producer. The results were rather stunning. For high-end routers sold into the U.S. market, R&D constituted between

20 and 25 percent of their total cost, so every 5 percent saving in R&D would generate a 1 percent margin improvement. Engineers in the United States earned roughly three to ten times what their counterparts earned in China—a range of US$50,000 to US$150,000 compared with US$7,000 to US$14,000. The engineers in China worked longer hours, nearly 20 percent longer on average. However, they were less efficient than those in the United States, and so the Chinese operation needed more engineers. Taking all these factors into account, in the end, the American company spent nearly five times more than the Chinese company to develop a comparable product. When a Chinese firm saves 80 percent on its R&D in this product category, it starts with an overall cost advantage of 16 percent from its R&D alone. A company needs extremely persuasive arguments for it to forgo that sort of advantage by keeping its R&D in its developed home markets.

Research and Development Is the Same but Different in China

The achievements of pioneers such as P&G, Motorola, General Electric, Colgate, and General Motors provide lessons for other MNCs to follow as they beef up their commitment to R&D in China. In each case, successful companies took what they knew how to do elsewhere in the world and tailored practices and processes to fit within the constraints found in China today—or to take advantage of the opportunities found there. They did not reinvent the wheel: they adapted it.

Product winners in China built development operations that resemble in many ways similar operations in the United States or Europe. For instance, P&G's market research and product development organizations in China are organized similarly to parallel organizations elsewhere, are staffed with people who have the same skills, and do what their counterparts do anywhere else in the world. They conduct customer research, crunch quantitative analyses, and do sophisticated modeling. They convene focus groups and go into customers' homes to better understand on-site how consumers use products. They exploit global tools and frameworks to glean insights required for product breakthroughs. The product development process at P&G involves a standardized set of activities to qualify and launch products and is done the same way in P&G businesses around the globe, including China. Engineers and designers are willing to push the envelope based on these insights, whether on product-line extensions or fundamental product redesigns. And they prototype and test products for consumer acceptance before the company finally launches them.

But look more closely and you see the differences that separate top-performing execution in R&D in China from good-enough execution. As mentioned in the previous chapter, companies can't access the kind of market information in China that is readily available in more mature markets. Not only does that hinder how they develop market-product strategies, but also it hinders how they develop new products themselves, such as understanding at an actionable level what will appeal to consumers and what won't. But if information is difficult to gather, moving from data to insight is even more challenging. The market research firms that elsewhere would be capable of generating the required analysis have yet to develop such capabilities in China.

The head of innovation for a large multinational company with R&D operations in China pointed out that market research firms here—in addition to being far fewer than you would find in developed markets—in general act only as "arms and legs" to an MNC marketing group, unable to structure research and produce insights that comparable firms do in developed markets.

Also, in the United States and Europe there are more and better third-party design firms with real market knowledge than MNCs will find in China. At the same time, he said, the competition is so tough that his company has to "turn out roughly ten times as many SKUs here as we do in the U.S."[2]

With higher demands and fewer external resources on which to rely, companies in China are forced to do more in-house. P&G has developed very sophisticated capabilities in China to conduct its own research, analyze it, develop insights from it, and carry insights through to commercialization.

Analysts say that the techniques P&G's marketers and product design teams in China use to gather information would be familiar to marketers worldwide, but teams here must learn how to take what they can get to identify how consumers and competitors are behaving. In other words, marketers at MNCs in China, such as P&G, have to live with less certainty and less science than marketing and product development professionals in developed nations typically do. What this means is that companies serious about product development in China will, over time, build a proprietary capability: a deep understanding of the needs and behaviors of various Chinese segments (and how they are evolving) in every category they compete in, based on limited streams of data and insights born of trial and error.

In China, a number of multinational technology, pharmaceutical, and product companies, including P&G, have forged partnerships with universities and research programs to augment their capabilities. (Chinese universities frequently trumpet these arrangements in news stories.) These partnerships essentially provide additional leverage in the effort to cut through uncertainty. But it also means that development managers in China need slightly different skills than their colleagues in the United

States and Europe, namely, a more practiced ability to manage research partnerships, to keep a closer eye on outcomes, and to guard intellectual property. (The dilemma of intellectual property is discussed later in this chapter.)

What this adds up to is world-class standards for execution. Market leaders don't have development operations in China that perform at lower standards just because they are in China, constrained in ways that are unique to China. On the contrary, aspirations for their performance are set very high. To achieve these ambitious expectations, they don't try to reinvent the development wheel in China—they could never succeed at developing (as P&G does, for instance) one winning product after another if they tried to operate with bespoke processes and systems. Rather, they succeed because they take already proven processes, systems, and practices and adapt them as needed for this market.

Achieving Lower Costs

Product developers in China place great emphasis on keeping product costs low. P&G researchers in China will tell you that they spend more time and attention on reducing product cost than do their colleagues back home. Researchers and executives at other companies say the same: designing to low cost could emerge in the years ahead as a capability that can be leveraged to advantage when developing products in other markets. Certainly the seeds of these skills are already here.

To contain costs, good product developers in China resist pressure to design to specs that meet branding guidelines set in development operations outside China. They develop specs to compete in the local market, not to meet global market expectations.

Even P&G product developers in China detour from the company's standard development operating procedure to cut costs on packaging, for instance, or other product features in order to keep costs low and thereby reach a broader number of buyers with a product.

Sometimes, rigid adherence to globally established R&D processes—or branding interference from headquarters—can get in the way. We have seen instances in which developers, trying to accommodate branding directions from headquarters, create packaging that is thicker than needed for China's markets, or printed in a special ink that adheres to global brand standards but is unnecessarily costly when used in China. Also, although China abounds with good-quality, low-cost materials—both for the product and the packaging—overspecifying makes it more difficult to leverage these sources of cost advantage. Why use an imported component if a local one will be sufficient?

Companies in China can also design products to be manufactured at lower costs. Chinese manufacturers competing with the MNCs frequently have the advantage of lower capital expenditures. With the rapid growth of local capacity, many Chinese industries have developed low-cost volume manufacturing processes—using people rather than automation—that produce goods at comparable quality with up to 50 percent less capital involved. Moreover, even for the capital costs they do incur, Chinese companies achieve significant savings by employing local equipment, design, and construction.

For instance, one unexpected advantage in China is its large network of design institutes, across every manufacturing industry, originally set up along Soviet lines to ensure central planning for large projects. These were "centers of excellence" in the planned economy for the part of the economy they served. With their privatization and the elimination of many of their bureaucratic clients, these institutes are now upgrading their capabilities and developing and commercializing local process technologies. They excel at maximizing the cost advantages of local labor, as opposed to automation. In their designs, it makes sense to substitute labor-intensive local equipment, which can lead to up to 20 percent savings in equipment costs.

The point is that multinational companies have rarely taken advantage of this unique opportunity to design products for manufacturability in plants that do not have to look like MNC factories elsewhere in the world. They can take more advantage of opportunities to avoid loading on features that will require new plants to be built or special equipment to be imported from Europe or the United States and installed in plants. In other words, they can produce to the local cost structure—and this begins with design.

As mentioned in chapter 1, China is ripe terrain for companies to implement design-to-cost (DTC) practices. Toyota pioneered this development approach, which involves starting with a premium version of a product and removing features to cut costs. This forces designers to make critical cost trade-offs early in the design process. Global manufacturers have found it difficult to get their development organizations in developed markets to move to DTC approaches, which require very different ways of thinking through development, different analyses, and different processes. Greenfield development operations in China aren't yet set in their ways, and Chinese managers are more receptive to new ways to reduce costs.

One way companies in China could get developers to start adopting this practice is to get them focused on distinguishing between "premium needs," served only by high-end products, and "generic needs" met across the product range. For instance, Johnson & Johnson was the first MNC in China to introduce midpriced women's sanitary protection products, which provided the generic benefit of leakage protection but did not claim superior comfort or absorption, benefits that were reserved for the premium range.

Jorgen Clausen, CEO of Danfoss, recognized the need for designers in China to have latitude to make design decisions on the ground if costs were to be kept in check. "Low-cost products [for Chinese customers] must be designed from scratch, something our European engineers can't easily do. They don't have the right mentality and would set excessively high standards for even the smallest details, ending up with an over-engineered and too expensive product."[3]

Danfoss has established R&D centers in China for refrigeration, air-conditioning, and heating products. They are developing products for Chinese customers, but Clausen believes these products can also be low-cost platforms for new products that can then be tailored for developed markets—resulting in products that cost less to develop (than in Europe) for European customers, too. "I was visiting one of our R&D units in China recently," Clausen reflected. "And I looked over the shoulder of an engineer. On her screen I recognized a product I didn't think was being designed in China. Oh yes, she explained, she was running the project together with one guy in Germany, one in Slovakia, and one in Iowa."

Finally, there are two other China-specific angles to product development that multinational companies are learning. First, companies have to work more closely with their suppliers to get products developed than they typically do in the United States or Europe. Operating staff must closely monitor suppliers to ensure that things get made on time and according to spec. This often requires visiting the suppliers' factories frequently. Even after the prototype is complete, companies or their production agents stay in constant contact with the manufacturer to ensure ongoing, timely production. Before a product is released into mass production, a final set of samples absolutely must be made and reviewed by the product development group before mass production is authorized. All this oversight has to be built into processes.

The second issue involves pilot testing. Pilot testing is critical—and smart MNC product companies use pilot testing as market experiments. They are more experimental than they are at home—learning, in this uncertain and fluid environment, is a fundamental skill for good execution. Companies such as P&G and Motorola test products in cities of varied tiers, or levels of wealth, to gauge how customers in wealthier, more cosmopolitan coastal cities react and how customers in the inland towns do as well. Invariably the products run better in some Chinese markets than others, but it is critical to learn why this is so, and to what degree. At this stage of the game in China, developing proprietary customer insights is enormously valuable. When companies know enough from these experiments to target markets, they can concentrate resources and launch aggressively. P&G lines up its sales force and distributors to run with a product and provides them with saturated media coverage.

Safeguarding Intellectual Property

When multinational companies consider starting R&D in China, one of their most common concerns involves intellectual property (IP) protection. Surveys of MNCs across China as well as discussions with companies that are not yet here indicate this is a top concern. In 2004, for example, Chery Automobile launched the Chery QQ, a car that looked remarkably similar to the Chevrolet Spark. The Spark itself is based on the Daewoo Matiz minicar. General Motors purchased Daewoo's assets in 2002, and GM Daewoo licensed the Matiz design to the joint venture that GM has with SAIC and Wuling, which makes the Spark. Chery had been negotiating a licensing agreement (unsuccessfully) with Daewoo prior to the GM transaction. GM has pointed to similarities in body structure and interior and exterior design between the two vehicles, but Chery denies that it has copied anything and has never been found guilty of copying GM's intellectual property. The year after Chery launched it, the QQ outsold the Spark in China. More recently, Honda sued a Chinese automobile manufacturer it accused of copying Honda's CR-V sport utility vehicle.

Protecting intellectual property *is* an issue. Culturally, intellectual property has not had the value in China that it has had in the West. For years, the mind-set of people has been to copy or model success: it works and is a good idea, so I'll do it too. (Less value has been placed on intangibles of all sorts in China.) These lingering cultural and mind-set issues hamper broad enforcement of IP laws. In addition, the Chinese judicial system is still developing. The legal profession in China formed only in the past fifteen years and, as such, the level of professional experience is understandably lower than in the West. Many lawyers have a military background rather than any professional legal training.

Still, the IP enforcement system has been gradually tightening. In 1949, China's communist rulers abolished the country's existing patent laws and instead established laws that claimed state ownership of invention rights. By the 1970s, however, China began to reform IP protections, and it joined global IP and trade organizations such as the World Intellectual Property Organization (WIPO) and the General Agreement on Tariffs and Trade (GATT) during the 1980s and early 1990s. When China joined the World Trade Organization (WTO), it agreed to comply with a number of multilateral international treaties and agreements on intellectual property, and pledged to step up enforcement of IP rights. Since then, China has implemented a number of laws and regulations to better safeguard IP ownership rights.[4]

China's enforcement of IP rights has been a matter of some controversy and dispute. Chinese courts have been slow to take up infringement claims, but an increasing number of civil and criminal IP trials have been held—more each year—and many suits have been found in favor of the foreign company. Then again, some were not. Chery itself was a government-owned company when it launched the QQ, and China's State Intellectual Property Office (SIPO)—China's equivalent to the U.S. Patent and Trade Office—sided with Chery and against GM in initial findings. In consumer electronics, every new product will generate—quite quickly—a host of lower-cost but remarkably similar (in function and sometimes design) rival domestic products. Piracy rates remain high.

Still, given the lure of Chinese markets, more and more MNCs seem to be willing to gamble that the tide has turned on IP protection and are willing to risk more IP exposure in China—particularly by engaging in R&D activities. In the pharmaceutical industry, for instance, most big global companies have been slow to open R&D centers, citing IP theft as the primary reason for staying away. But companies such as Novartis and Roche recently decided the situation has changed, and opened centers in China. Novartis even formed a partnership with the government-run Shanghai Institute for Materia Medica to identify drug compounds derived from traditional Chinese medicines. Roche opened a Shanghai R&D facility, only its fifth globally, employing forty scientists, at the start of 2005. Other MNCs still balk at the idea.

For those companies that have made R&D commitments in China, the opportunities to strengthen government relationships can be significant. National policy to encourage innovation uses IP protection as a progress metric. Multinational companies that are investing in local innovation are seen as helping meet these policy aspirations. As such, the Chinese government has made more than just a verbal commitment to improve IP protection: it has an incentive to attract more multinational company R&D. If it follows the example set by other countries and ensures better IP protection, the government could help develop local industry. In Japan, for example, the government introduced patent protection for pharmaceuticals in 1976. Significant growth in R&D activity followed, and since 1986 the Japanese pharmaceutical industry has been a net exporter of technology.

Companies should not base their decision to do R&D in China solely on an assessment of the state of legal protection as compared with government protections for IP found in the United States and Europe. Although government support for better IP protection continues to develop, companies can and must take steps of their own to maximize protection of their IP. Based on our discussions with a number of multinational and domestic companies in China, we think IP protection should not be viewed as strictly a legal issue. Indeed, it isn't strictly a legal issue elsewhere in the world, either, but in China companies are focusing too much of their attention on government solutions, and not enough on solutions within their control. Indeed, those companies that try to protect themselves solely through legal procedures are not effective.

Companies would be better served to consider their IP shield as something like a pyramid of protections (figure 4-1). At the bottom of the pyramid are a set of legal actions companies can take to aggressively defend against IP theft. For instance, they should register their patents, trademarks, and copyrights with

FIGURE 4-1

A pyramid of intellectual property protection

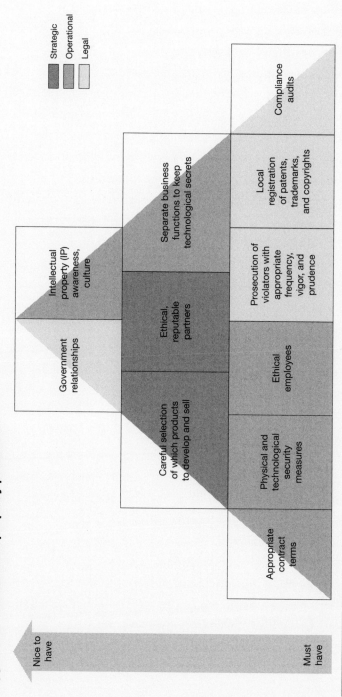

SIPO. This may seem obvious, but many companies have neglected to do so, either in a rush to enter the market or in the false belief that it is not worth the bother.

Registering a patent discloses information about the invention and about the manufacturing and design processes involved in the invention. But if a company has already registered the patent in another country, this information is available anyway. In China, infringers have obtained registered information and then violated patents, and there is some concern that registering a patent in China only makes this information more readily available to infringers. But companies have limited enforcement protection for patents in China unless they are registered, so companies will need to assess the trade-offs on patents, trademarks, and copyrights on a case-by-case basis. Chinese laws also require applying for patents at SIPO first for certain inventions made in China before registering them in other countries, but processes also exist for companies to register a patent through international structures. China also has different kinds of patents that companies can apply for, with different life cycles. Needless to say, companies should assess and make patent decisions with the advice of counsel familiar with Chinese patent law.[5]

Registering patents is one thing; getting patents enforced or trade secrets protected is another. Multinational companies can—and do—file complaints with the government, initiate civil suits, or lodge criminal complaints with the Public Security Bureau if they believe trade secrets have been stolen or patents infringed. But legal battles and weaponry alone aren't enough to protect critical IP in China. As we have seen in many high-profile cases, pressing for prosecution can get the company tangled in lengthy and costly legal disputes—with highly unpredictable outcomes. Litigation can, in some cases, harm important local government or regulator relationships that the company has put time and effort into building (and still not recover the lost IP). The decision to press for civil or criminal legal action should be thought through carefully; sometimes it makes sense to be aggressive in pressing one's case, sometimes not.[6]

Companies can more successfully leverage legal tactics when combined with other "must have" operational moves as the foundation of the pyramid. This building block of protection is about putting into place measures to keep sensitive information away from potential patent infringers and pirates. Steps companies take in this regard include implementing appropriate physical and technological security measures, hiring ethical employees, and ensuring that appropriate contract terms are written into supplier and employee agreements. Some MNCs have carefully defined what information is sensitive and what isn't, and have defined procedures for how to (and who can) handle more sensitive information. A few companies also keep sensitive information in restricted areas, conduct random security checks on information handling within the organization, and use surveillance equipment or firewalls to prevent file transfer outside the company's walls.

Employees are a critical line of operational defense in the protection of IP. Companies such as GE screen all job candidates for high ethical standards. Other multinational companies in China recruit local employees with international work and educational experience, which they hope ensures a common understanding for the value of intellectual property. (For instance, one global pharmaceutical executive told us that his company looks to hire local R&D scientists with foreign PhDs and work experience because in his view working overseas engenders a greater appreciation of the value of intellectual property.) GE and others conduct employee training sessions on IP at orientation and in intervals thereafter for follow-up reinforcement of key IP protection messages. Also, some companies ask employees to sign documents stating that they understand company policies on handling IP. One pharmaceutical company reinforces IP awareness by requiring employees to sign noncompete clauses, which prevent employees from serving competitors for up to three years after leaving the company.

In addition to these basic blocking-and-tackling moves, companies can put into place a second level of protections—typically a set of issues undertaken by more senior managers. For instance, a critical aspect of IP protection is deciding with whom to partner in China. Executives from the companies that best protect their IP carefully select their partnerships in China. The most successful companies conduct due diligence on potential partners before entering into contracts or supplier agreements. To ensure similar respect for IP, they choose partners based on their reputation and ethics, not just on business rationale. A company with a good reputation and brand in China is much less likely to engage in IP infringement, because the advantages it gains from this reputation would be put at risk. Of course, companies also press for appropriate contract terms with suppliers to ensure effective IP protection, and audit the compliance of partners frequently and regularly—two activities we consider first-level, foundational practices for ensuring IP protection. A leading high-tech components manufacturer, for instance, routinely verifies that the number of components delivered to its customers matches the number in products subsequently sold in the market. By doing so, this company has a way to identify possible leakage and is ready to take prompt legal action if necessary.

Other multinational companies have taken equity stakes in select suppliers to keep any potential for piracy at bay. This is quickly becoming a best practice among the global automotive OEMs operating in China. Taking an equity stake in a top supplier ensures better alignment of interests and facilitates processes for monitoring compliance.

At the second layer of the pyramid, there are also some strategic decisions companies can make to gain better IP protection. For instance, is there some IP they would rather keep outside of China for the near term? Some companies have decided to withhold their most innovative products or portions of product development from the Chinese market altogether. In some cases, these companies will introduce a lower-margin product or more mature products, where there is less risk if the product is pirated. One large equipment manufacturer designs and develops hardware in China but produces the related software, which is the most valuable IP, abroad. By separating functions and technological details in this way, the manufacturer maintains better control over its intellectual property.

Finally, the top layer of the pyramid is comprised of a couple of capstone managerial actions. Many companies successfully build government relationships as another way to support IP protection. One high-end electronics speaker company reported counterfeiting activity to the local government, hired private investigators to conduct raids, and worked with local government officials to orchestrate public demonstrations. The combination of tactics helped this company build awareness of the value of the brand and technology so that it curbed counterfeiting activity for five years following prosecution.

Also, building a significant presence in China and a strong brand image is an increasingly formidable barrier to IP theft. Having a large organization is China is a deterrent to potential infringers. If you're there in force, you are a higher-risk target for them than companies with minimal presence. Infringers know that companies with large organizations in China are able to spot problems faster and are potentially better at monitoring compliance. Having a strong brand image also heightens the risks for pirates because their activities are more visible in the market with consumers as well as monitors. Auto OEMs are going so far as to mark components in a vehicle with the OEM's logo, transforming a part into a branded element of the product.

Although theft of intellectual property is certainly a risk in China, companies can take steps to better manage IP—and in the meantime build the research and development capabilities they will need to succeed in China's new markets. How the products designed for China's markets are made in China is the topic of our next chapter.

CHAPTER FIVE

The Next Advantage for Manufacturing

You've picked the markets in which you want to fight and plotted a game plan for entering them. You've researched target segments and consumer needs. You're developing new products calculated to meet those needs that incorporate winning features and are designed to be competitively priced. But can you manufacture them profitably? Can your factory meet order dates reliably? Can you deliver quality products?

Manufacturing is at the very core of China's boom. Arbitraging China's low labor costs, multinational companies have been quick to open plants in China to manufacture products for this market, and sometimes for markets elsewhere in the world. (However, many global companies may not be doing enough manufacturing in China, and they certainly aren't doing enough sourcing, as we explain in chapter 6.) But low labor costs have frequently excused a multitude of manufacturing performance deficiencies that companies would never allow in their operations elsewhere in the world. The excuse runs as follows: It's different in China. We have to accept less maturity and work around it.

A witch's brew of competitive pressures—including increasing demand, the need to scale up manufacturing of new products, pricing pressures on existing offerings, rising commodity prices, and the move by some leading rivals to improve manufacturing performance—is pushing companies to stop making excuses. The bar on execution is rising. Yes, China is different, but the pressure is on manufacturing managers to nevertheless begin to meet world-class global operating standards. As we've argued in the previous chapters, they need to stop seeing the differences in China as impediments to top-flight execution and instead see them as merely variations on a theme—operational excellence in a China kind of way.

The story of how one company overhauled its manufacturing operations is illustrative. Let us introduce you to Bill Haag, vice president of international operations at the Cleveland, Ohio–based manufacturing company Preformed Line Products (PLP). We are inside the company's primary factory in China, a 60,000-square-foot plant located in a small industrial park about an hour's drive outside Beijing. Haag and Wu Yu, managing director of PLP China, are showing off all the physical changes they've made to the operations since we had last visited just two months earlier.[1]

One can immediately see the improvement: where once the factory floor had been a clutter of inventory, finished products, damaged goods, and machines and teams crowding each other, it is now a portrait of order, with space divided equally for three long production lines, fed by material provided just in time from well-ordered shelves of inventory, and in turn feeding finished product to a preshipping work area that debouched to a loading dock.

Haag has stopped beside a machine to answer a visitor's question. "This facility now produces more product per piece of equipment than any of our other facilities outside of the U.S.," he says. "Right now 50 percent of our production is for domestic Chinese customers, and 50 percent is for export around the world. We'd like both to grow about 20 percent a year."

PLP makes equipment that telecommunications, communications, and power companies use to secure cable to telephone poles or underground lines. It is a midsize business, with operations and customers in many countries throughout the world. PLP opened a factory in China in 1996, in a joint venture with a domestic Chinese electric power company. PLP's factory—which took advantage of very low labor rates—provided the company with a cost advantage that allowed for competing on cost against rivals in global markets. At the same time, demand by domestic telecommunications and communications customers grew quickly. And although PLP's operations in China were not anywhere near as efficient as its best operations elsewhere, they did not need to be: China's low costs trumped all.

PLP's factory was, from the start, in much better shape than other factories in China. As we've seen in factory after factory in China, including the China operations of some of the world's most accomplished manufacturers, waste is prevalent: machines sit idle, inventory piles up, and bottlenecks choke production. Parts deliveries from suppliers arrive late. Defect rates on components run high.

No one questions the need to improve execution. Now that so many companies produce in China, the low cost of labor once enjoyed by the few confers little advantage. But companies can gain relative advantages anew by dramatically boosting performance. Operating executives of MNCs know what they should do to improve their plants. There is no secret solution: manufacturers around the world have spent the last twenty years implementing and refining such tools and approaches as lean, quality, and Six Sigma to push their operations into a fine groove. Best practices in manufacturing are widely understood; the question is how to apply them in China.

PLP found answers to that question. For PLP, the problem that piqued management to focus on execution was a capacity crunch. By 2004, the factory was becoming bogged down in long production runs for export orders—orders big enough to efficiently fill a shipping container or two. But domestic orders were backing up, and customers were not happy. Lead times for domestic orders rose to fourteen days. In this sector, lead time is a competitive advantage. PLP's products are low tech, and they are competing against a host of rivals (including some from China). Product knowledge and cost are important to customers, but so is a provider's ability to fill a big order quickly and reliably. "Every system in the business [in China] was under stress," Haag recalls. "The computer system, the maintenance and quality systems— everything was overloaded. Our people and our managers were overloaded." And still demand was growing.

PLP initially considered a more traditional solution: build another plant in China, buy more equipment, and hire more people. But PLP had by then successfully introduced lean techniques to do more with less in its U.S. operations, and wondered if it could do the same in China. Lean techniques aim to identify and eliminate root causes of waste. Implementing these techniques in China, however, presents challenges that can easily trip up even companies well versed in the discipline. Chinese managers, often recently promoted from the shop floor, lack not only crucial skills in problem solving, coaching, and performance management but also the industry-specific expertise needed to diagnose complex technical problems accurately and develop effective solutions rapidly. Relentless growth in many industries means that because factories constantly scramble to fill orders and expand capacity, they have little time to refine their production processes. Furthermore, high employee turnover undercuts the continuity that is central to the use of lean techniques.

PLP chose to tackle its execution problem head-on. Beginning in mid-2005, PLP initiated a fairly quick and intensive program to adapt lean tools to its China plant—carefully tailoring what worked in the United States to the realities of China. It had to work around equipment, quality, and training limitations, deal with cultural differences that undercut employee performance and problem solving, address supplier deficiencies, and tackle a legion of other challenges. But it did it. One year after launching the program, PLP's lead times had dropped from fourteen to three days, capacity utilization rose from 28 to 50 percent, and on-time delivery rates rose from 66 to over 80 percent. Demand continues to rise. "Bringing in new ideas from the West, such as lean, and having them understood, accepted, and adopted here is a big challenge," PLP China's Wu Yu told us. "But it can be done."

Some companies in China today are content to grow by adding machines and labor. This approach is certainly an option: factories typically ramp up in a few weeks or months in China rather than the many months or years needed elsewhere. Investment budgets are huge, and companies feel tremendous pressure to build whatever capacity they can. But a growing number of MNCs manufacturing in China are not content with this. They are also setting high aspirations for productivity—beginning to drive for performance levels comparable to the company's operations elsewhere in the world. The leaders among these companies are rapidly improving execution by adopting globally recognized lean manufacturing techniques, such as pull systems or *poka yoke* (a Japanese term that means designing foolproof production steps to reduce the number of defects). Toyota introduced lean techniques to the rest of the world during the 1980s, and is now introducing them in the company's factories in China. Auto industry suppliers, such as Delphi and Lear, are also on the lean bandwagon in China.

Alcoa has already earned some bragging rights in this area. Alcoa began implementing its highly successful Alcoa Business System (ABS) at its Shanghai plant in 1998. The ABS, modeled on Toyota's all-encompassing approach to integrated, lean operations, helped rocket the company to a leadership position in its sector during the 1990s. Its approach to lean—with some adaptation—worked in China as well. Within six years of beginning the transformation of its manufacturing plant in Shanghai, Alcoa managed to shorten lead times at the plant by 30 to 50 percent, double its sales volume (both for domestic sales and export), and greatly reduce inventories. Based on what it learned at the Shanghai plant about how to successfully adapt global standards such as lean, Alcoa has begun to implement world-class execution standards in its plants in Bohai and Kunshan.

General Electric introduced Six Sigma in its eight lighting division plants in 1996. Domestic Chinese companies are also rapidly adopting global standards such as Six Sigma or lean to improve performance. Baosteel, for instance, is in the midst of an aggressive program to implement hundreds of lean- and Six Sigma–based improvement programs across its operations. In its two hot rolling mills, for instance, the company now sets hundreds of specific production and technology development targets, and hits more than 90 percent of them. Throughput at the mills has been exceeding design capacity by 30 percent in recent years.

The company also set high aspirations for performance improvement: for equipment systems, "three times 10 percent reductions" is the goal, says Zhao Zhouli, vice general manager (and the executive responsible for manufacturing) at Baosteel. "Ten percent reduction in breakdown time, 10 percent down in maintenance costs, and 10 percent down in labor load of maintenance."

Opportunities to Improve Execution

The headroom for improving manufacturing productivity in China is considerable. Chinese factories, for example, usually repair or scrap faulty products as they come off the assembly line rather than produce them properly in the first place. Quality control at each stage of production relies mainly on the experience of individual workers, not on rigorous and widely used statistical tools (such as Six Sigma), which are poorly understood and incorrectly applied in China, so that defect rates are high. At one telecommunications equipment maker, for example, we found that only 68 percent of all printed-circuit boards passed inspection recently, well below the company's target of 80 to 90 percent. (Ninety percent is the norm in world-class plants such as ones run by this telecom giant elsewhere in the world.)

What's more, Chinese factories often make products in big batches, thereby creating large inventories of partly finished goods that are prone to damage because they lie around for lengthy periods. (This is true in many plants around the world where lean hasn't yet been fully embraced: manufacturing managers believe it is easier to make a big batch, shut the plant down, and then make another big batch. This is more wasteful than the one-piece flow approach of lean production.) The result is higher costs and late deliveries. Poor coordination between different steps in the production process often creates bottlenecks: at one manufacturer, workers spend 40 percent of their time waiting because of upstream delays.

Unfortunately, cultural norms often stand in the way of efforts to address these wasteful practices. Many Chinese managers celebrate success at the first sign of any minor improvement. They aren't accustomed to the kind of rigorous, long-term effort needed to make lean-manufacturing initiatives pay off. In addition, the hierarchical nature of Chinese organizations hinders the cooperation and joint decision making—across departmental boundaries, as well as up and down the chain of command—needed to solve the thorniest problems.

For companies that tackle waste successfully, the payoff can be significant. Inefficient work routines and poor equipment maintenance, for example, made one domestic steelmaker's mill run at only 60 percent of capacity. If that level rose to the industry benchmark—about 90 percent—the company's profits would increase by upward of US$100 million a year. Moreover, as mentioned in chapter 1, a McKinsey study of electronics factories found that wasteful practices and high defect rates reduced profits by 20 to 40 percent as compared with returns at world-class plants. If the survey's median factory (in terms of output) matched the top performers', profits would rise by about US$25 million a year.

Many benefits, such as reducing inventories and raising quality, require limited investment and have a short payback period, so the incentive to achieve them by using lean techniques is strong. To improve the likelihood of success, however, MNC operating executives in China must ensure that some key elements are in place. Managers and factory workers alike need a new intellectual tool set to solve complex problems and make smart changes in the way they work. Companies need better systems to set performance goals and measure the workers' ability to meet them. Finally, in a country where swift change is the norm, companies must focus the minds of their employees on the importance of constant long-term improvement.

Adapting Lean Techniques

In applying lean techniques, factories in China—whether MNC operations or domestic Chinese companies—use the same basic approach that factories elsewhere use. First, they typically establish specific goals based on what their customers want, determine the ideal production process for achieving those goals, and select and train managers who can implement the required changes on the factory floor. Then they run a pilot program demonstrating the effectiveness of lean operations and roll out the program across the entire factory, business unit, or company. A few of the most successful organizations have even linked their lean initiatives to their overall performance management systems.

Building Know-How

For the lean approach to succeed in China, companies must surmount many hurdles. The kind of focus on fine-tuning production systems that works well in places such as Stuttgart and Detroit tends to fall flat in Shenzhen and Shanghai, where steps in the production process are ill defined and the skills needed to understand and improve them are rare.

One way of filling the knowledge gap quickly is to tap outside experts. In China, this approach requires creativity because experienced production engineers are scarce. Companies can recruit retired engineers—a potential source of valuable technical knowhow—from Japan and Taiwan through local trade associations or other industry and personal networks. Richard Ru-Gin Chang, the founder of the Shanghai-based chip maker Semiconductor Manufacturing International Corporation (SMIC), recruited engineers largely through personal contacts at his former employers.

Companies can also use headhunters and advertisements to tap the increasingly large pool of technical specialists from places such as Taiwan, Singapore, and South Korea who are willing to work in China. At Asia Pulp & Paper, an Indonesian conglomerate that is the largest paper manufacturer in China, for example, several of the mill managers are Taiwanese expatriates. In addition, suppliers of factory equipment are sometimes willing to work closely with a manufacturer if the collaboration will help them develop new processes or products. The supplier's technicians often work the bugs out of machinery and production processes inside a manufacturer's own plant, for example, thereby providing valuable on-the-job training for shop-floor employees and supervisors. European equipment makers such as Danieli & C. Officine Meccaniche and SMS Demag, for instance, are transferring steelmaking expertise to their clients' workers by designing their latest equipment in concert with Chinese steel companies.

Yet raising the technical and problem-solving skills of frontline factory workers presents a special challenge because the knowledge base is often close to zero, and turnover is high. Training curriculums must be much simpler than they usually are in the factories of, say, Italy or Japan, and sessions must convene more frequently. Likewise, Chinese workers tend to learn faster from hands-on shop-floor exercises than from the theoretical classroom sessions typical elsewhere. The challenge calls for experienced instructors who can roll up their sleeves and overcome the cultural customs that often impede training.

One common challenge is getting several departments to solve problems together. Because of the rigid hierarchies of Chinese organizations, the general manager or some other senior official usually makes decisions that cut across a number of functions. But this approach is impractical in everyday circumstances on the factory floor. Take, as an example, a common situation: mechanical engineers, electrical-maintenance personnel, and machine operators must together learn to disassemble a piece of factory equipment in order to identify a problem's root cause. Savvy instructors can break down the barriers among the three groups by playing on the Chinese people's deep-seated sense of hierarchy and inherent sense of honor—often referred to as "face." If the instructors, whose position commands respect, begin to tear down the machine, the workers watching will soon join in to save face themselves and show their respect, even if this kind of participation conflicts with the departmental hierarchy.

Hierarchy must be addressed at other organizational levels as well. As PLP China's managing director, Wu Yu, noted, supervisors are more culturally at home in structures where they act as monitors. But when PLP began to implement lean techniques, Wu Yu wanted supervisors to become active problem solvers, not monitors. "This is very difficult in China," he said. "People here don't like to be challenged. In the West, people speak up and suggest ways to solve problems. In China they are less inclined to speak up and make a difference. They wait for the person above them to say what needs to be done. Supervisors like to say 'Do this' rather than get workers involved in problem solving, and workers typically don't give ideas to managers."

PLP found that short, focused kaizen events can help. (Kaizen events are a core part of the lean tool kit. They bring together production workers, supervisors, and managers in a collective problem-solving meeting.) Although kaizen events are typically several days long in the West, PLP kept some of them to a day or less, and limited the participation carefully, to better ensure outcomes that provided not only good ideas but also good learning experiences for workers. "It's taking time for these changes to happen," Wu Yu said.

Although the skill level of Chinese workers is generally low, their hunger to learn is typically high, for they know that developing skills is the route to better jobs. In a country where more than 40 percent of all manufacturing jobs are newly created or destroyed each year—compared with less than 20 percent in North America—workers have strong incentives to learn quickly.

Creating a Performance Culture

Chinese supervisors lack experience in managing performance. They tend to focus mainly on fighting fires and have little time to use systematic management tools. The failure to bear down on performance is also partly cultural; in general, the Chinese would prefer to avoid talking frankly with their peers about their personal performance. Yet to implement lean techniques, managing for performance is as critical as problem solving: identifying problems is one thing; applying disciplined remedies is another.

To change the behavior of such employees, companies must have a strong leader who drives change by setting clear targets and holding subordinates personally accountable. The leader is usually a CEO acting as a symbolic focal point of the improvement effort but can also be a department head backed up by upper management. The leader must implement a performance evaluation system that reinforces the aims of lean manufacturing. In factories in Japan or the United States, managers typically pick performance indicators (such as defect rates) and routinely determine whether individual workers meet their goals. In China, however, workers are liable to accept such a system more readily if it analyzes the performance of groups rather than individuals. An effective model would thus be to tie a worker's pay to a team's performance, with perhaps 20 percent of total compensation rising or falling with the team's progress (or failure) in meeting set goals. A few companies already take an even more aggressive approach: Baosteel, for instance, ties 40 percent of an average worker's—and 70 percent of a manager's—pay to performance.

Unfortunately, this approach can go awry if, as happens all too often in China, companies choose inappropriate performance goals. At the Chinese factory of one multinational cable manufacturer, nearly half the bonus pay of production workers was tied to the number of pieces they produced. The result was overproduction and wasteful stockpiles of finished inventory ranging from twenty to seventy days, depending on the product. Managers took the bold move of linking pay to a balanced set of incentives—with metrics such as quality and cleanliness as well as daily production targets—even though they initially thought that it would depress production. In fact, the company has almost doubled its capacity, dramatically reduced its stock of finished goods, and made its employees more satisfied with their work.

Making Sustainable Gains

One of the most difficult hurdles that multinational and domestic companies in China face in successfully introducing lean techniques is sustaining the long-term effort needed to break factory bottlenecks. The current tendency is to work furiously on many projects and hope that improvement will somehow result. In a society where leaders have exercised political power through the mass mobilization of the Cultural Revolution and the Great Leap Forward, getting large numbers of people to look as though they are actively following a consistent path often seems more important than genuine, measurable improvement. Chinese factories are still festooned with posters announcing the current Communist Party slogans. Superficial campaigns to improve quality or boost production take the place of an exacting focus on well-defined problems.

For lean programs to work in China, managers must find ways to adapt them to this tradition of mass mobilization. The success of pilot projects in tackling waste or improving quality must be widely trumpeted as a way of triggering momentum toward change. More than in Western plants, companies must train the workers who participate in these pilots to serve as a cadre of specialists spearheading the rollout of change throughout the plant or the company. A pilot project can demonstrate the benefits of lean manufacturing in a tangible way that is much more likely to convince skeptical factory workers than a more theoretical approach.

Simple improvements requiring few new skills send workers the powerful message that it is easy to learn smarter ways of performing even basic tasks. In the rolling mill of one steel plant, for example, the time needed to change the rolls that flatten metal into sheets fell by 50 percent (to ten minutes). This pilot project succeeded thanks to the introduction of simple changes such as replacing faulty components quickly and rescheduling the overhaul of other equipment to avoid interference with roll changes.

In addition to using pilots, companies must organize their communications and training exercises on a much larger scale than would be necessary in Japan or the West. In one organization of about four thousand employees, nearly half of the workforce received instruction in the basics of lean manufacturing over a three-month period just to lay the foundation for the practical work ahead. This kind of mass communication about the intent of a program is critical in setting high expectations for its success and motivating change. Making lean techniques the focus of everything from media reports to education dovetails nicely with the propensity of Chinese factories to celebrate activity. For senior managers, who are often concerned about the way lean manufacturing will affect their power, taking benchmarking trips to best-practice companies can help remove misconceptions.

Another complication in applying lean principles is the relentless, rapid pace of change in most factories in China today as manufacturers add new capacity and their product designs evolve. To cope, companies must give lean initiatives shorter time horizons than they have elsewhere and implement them more swiftly. Western companies tend to plan their programs and to identify pilot projects by asking themselves where they want to be in seven to ten years' time; in China, these plans must be updated every two or three years. The compressed time frame means that companies have just twelve to eighteen months to move from the pilot phase to the rollout of changes throughout the organization.

Such a demanding pace is possible in China because factory workers are less bound by traditional ways of working and are more adaptable to change than their counterparts in Europe, Japan, or North America. Nevertheless, companies in China can adopt lean techniques rapidly enough only if strong leaders set the direction, give workers the know-how they need, and establish effective incentives.

Finally, lean techniques can help a company shave its capital costs in China. China is manufacturing more and more of the world's goods. Every day, plants are reaching capacity and companies are putting new plants on the drawing board. As PLP discovered, adopting lean tools and techniques can help manufacturers make more (and better) use of what they have already, holding those new costs at bay. In our experience, looking at hundreds of plants in China, we believe there is 30 to 50 percent or even sometimes as much as 100 percent more capacity untapped inside a manufacturer's existing facilities.

Lean, in other words, is a vehicle for growth in China, in part because lean frees up capacity, and in part because the stabilization of production time and improvement of quality are a platform upon which companies can safely grow market share.

As competition intensifies in China's new markets, pressures will mount on companies to improve their execution in every aspect of manufacturing in China. Lean manufacturing approaches that have proven to boost productivity and quality in operations around the world will work in China too, when tailored to the local realities. Suppliers are a critical element in the manufacturing value chain in China—and globally—and we address this issue in the next chapter.

CHAPTER SIX

Getting More from
Sourcing More in China

Sourcing in China is a somewhat more holistic problem for
multinational companies to solve. Thus far in the book, we have
been moving in a straight line from identifying new markets and
segments in China to developing new products for them and then
to manufacturing those products. Sourcing is about managing
the suppliers that deliver materials and components to manufacturing plants and, in ideal situations, work in partnership with
manufacturing managers to incorporate their components or
subassemblies smoothly into the production process—and in
even more ideal instances, work with product developers to design components and products to cost and to manufacturability.
But MNCs in China not only source goods for their operations

there, but also buy goods, parts, or materials from Chinese suppliers (or foreign companies making products in China) to use in making products elsewhere in the world. Thus, managing supply isn't just about winning in new middle-class markets in China, it is also about winning globally.

As we've noted, the first principle for becoming world class at execution in China is to set aspirations high. Multinational companies are falling short against this aspiration in China—but even more so globally. That may seem to be an odd assertion on the face of it. After all, there can't be a person left in Europe or America who does not know that China is a key supplier to retailers and businesses in developed markets. Consumers know full well that they are able to buy more because they pay less for goods made in China, including clothing and shoes with "made in China" labels, tools and high-tech products sold under global brand names, and cars that are assembled in the United States and Germany with parts manufactured in China's plants. The Chinese know it, too—their standard of living also rises on the wave of this trade.

But what the man or woman on the street in Boise, Bremen, and Beijing probably doesn't know is this: global companies could source substantially more from China than they now do. We recently completed an assessment of procurement operations at thirty-nine MNCs in China, across ten different industries, including auto parts manufacturing, high tech, and retailing. We found that these MNCs are typically sourcing for global use only about one-third of the goods they believe they could potentially source in China, and are getting only about one-quarter of the potential savings. This is because they know they're getting better prices than at home, but don't yet know just how low prices in China can be. One retailer was getting 20 to 30 percent savings sourcing in China. After a few years, the retailer introduced a reverse auction system in China—and saw one of its primary Chinese suppliers quickly drop prices another 20 to 30 percent in competition to keep the retailer's business. Additionally, while volumes have been increasing, it takes time to wring out costs. Based on current trajectories for sourcing growth in these companies, we estimate they will still be sourcing only half what they could by the end of 2008, and will still not be getting anywhere near the full savings potential of what they source in China by then.

Global companies are leaving tremendous value on the table. They simply aren't setting their aspirations high enough for what their sourcing operations can achieve for the corporation, both in China and globally. Certainly there are numerous procurement and supply management challenges to face, such as identifying good suppliers; overcoming language and cultural barriers; boosting suppliers' quality; ensuring reliable deliveries; managing supply chain inventory; communicating with engineering, design, and procurement managers in corporate headquarters; and overcoming logistics hurdles. Over the years, MNC supply management and procurement managers in China have solved some of these problems, but new ones continue to pop up—as is always the case in sourcing, no matter where in the world you're doing it. Executives of MNCs in China know that the local sourcing challenges aren't the real reason why their company's sourcing levels are just a trickle of what they could be. The real reason is that aspirations aren't set high enough, from global headquarters on down, and consequently the company isn't putting in the focus or the resources to be successful. In China sourcing, MNCs are underachieving. That's not world-class execution.

Let's take a moment to parse our terms, however. A company such as PLP, which we highlighted in the last chapter for its manufacturing achievements, is making products in China for Chinese customers. So are a legion of other MNCs such as Caterpillar,

P&G, Danfoss, Motorola, General Motors, and Fuji Xerox. A subset of companies manufacturing in China for Chinese markets are also manufacturing products (or subassemblies) in China for global markets—PLP is one of them. To manufacture these products or components, the MNCs tap local suppliers and the China-based plants of their global suppliers.

Multinational companies also buy components or goods from Chinese plants and ship them to plants elsewhere in the world, where the parts are incorporated into products that are assembled and sold in global markets. The U.S. auto OEMs, for instance, buy some rubber parts for automobiles from Chinese suppliers. These parts are incorporated into cars or car subassemblies being put together in Mexico or the United States.

Moreover, some global companies, such as Panasonic, and many others, buy finished goods from Chinese suppliers and sell them under their own brands in developed markets. And, of course, retailers such as Wal-Mart and Carrefour are buying an increasingly broad range of goods—from televisions, tools, and toys to clothing, cookware, and crockery—from China's factories (whether domestic or foreign-owned) for store shelves in China and elsewhere around the world.

Finally, MNCs in China (and some not in China) also buy indirect goods—such as office supplies and furniture, copiers, corporate cell phones, and the like—from domestic Chinese companies. Sometimes these are for their offices and plants in China, sometimes for properties elsewhere in the world, and sometimes both.

That is a very broad range of opportunities for sourcing. There is need for improvement across the entire range. Whether buying components in China from local suppliers to use in factories in China or to ship for use overseas, MNCs are buying less than they could and paying more than they should.

Consider the level of China sourcing that is possible in the auto sector. China is the world's second-largest market for autos, and as of 2006 became the third-largest *producer* of autos behind the United States and Japan. All the major global OEMs are in China, along with all the major global auto parts makers, and they are competing in China (and soon globally) with world-class domestic parts makers and OEMs. But the international OEMs are still only buying a trickle of parts for use in products assembled elsewhere in the world (much less making whole cars in China for global markets).[1] Most of the China-made auto components that the international OEMs purchase are for cars they make and sell with their joint venture partners *in China*. China-made auto parts amount to just 2 percent of the U.S. parts sector alone.

Yes, there are impediments to increased sourcing. First, parts made for cars in China are different from parts made for cars in the United States. Cars built for a China market are frequently low-cost, stripped-down models that might not appeal to U.S. consumers and probably would not pass U.S. safety regulations. Second, many car parts are subject to frequent engineering changes, so making them in China increases the management complexity of supplying them to the United States; there are also risks associated with having a supply chain that stretches halfway around the world. Yet the PC and laptop computer sector faced very similar supply chain challenges during the 1990s and overcame the challenges; today nearly all notebook computers are made in China. If automakers can find solutions to the challenges of China sourcing in their sector, there is an enormous economic opportunity for OEMs to better integrate the sourcing they already do in China with their broader global operations to lower the cost of cars assembled and sold in other markets.

With few exceptions, global retailers could lift their aspirations for putting Chinese goods on global store shelves. One retailer shifted nearly US$300 million in purchases to China over nine months, yielding an average of 25 percent savings on a total landed cost basis. Three years later it is purchasing about US$1 billion worth of goods from Chinese manufacturers, and feels that it could do considerably more. Retailers frequently are sourcing volumes at the low end of what is possible for them. Moreover, many retailers source too many categories through agents. By our estimates, retail chains in the United States and Europe save an average of 15 to 35 percent across categories by purchasing goods sourced in China through intermediary buyers (called agents). The few retailers that do some of their own buying in China directly from the manufacturers (thereby disintermediating the middle market) save at least an additional 10 to 15 percent above what agents get there, and often more than that.

The gap between what's possible and what's being done can be considerable. One *Fortune* 500 company that sells wholesale and retail goods does a limited amount of sourcing in China. We looked closely at a representative sample of more than two dozen of the company's SKUs (which the company's executives helped to identify), and found that sourcing these SKUs in China could produce savings of over 20 percent on a total landed cost basis (even factoring in increased shipping, insurance, and inventory costs). Extrapolating these findings, the company realized that if it systematically sourced from China the relevant product categories involved, the company's net income could increase by 50 percent. Similarly, a large American retailer estimates that if it direct sourced "clean wins" in China, saving a conservative 10 percent on the cost of these goods, it could boost the company's net income by at least 30 percent.

A global industrial company that does some manufacturing in China recently estimated that its China sourcing roughly amounted to nearly 10 percent of global cost of goods sold. If it tripled the amount of sourcing it did in China, figuring an average savings of 20 percent on what is sourced here, the company's earnings before interest, taxes, depreciation, and amortization (EBITDA) could rise from 9 to 14 percent. That was eye-opening for executives. Then they realized that China sourcing could be the single biggest lever to increase the company's profitability over the next twenty-four to thirty-six months. As we write this, they have given the program a green light.

The opportunity lies in boosting the volume of direct and indirect goods flowing into an MNC's global supply chain from Chinese plants. A handful of MNCs are lifting their aspirations, and over the next few years will serve as models to the others. General Electric, for instance, set its sights in 2002 on doubling sales from its various businesses in China to US$5 billion by 2005 and to sourcing US$5 billion in components and goods from China by the same target date—a very aggressive target. The company hit its sales target, but achieved only three-fifths of its sourcing target at that time. In 2003, GE opened its US$64 million China Technology Center in Shanghai's Zhangjiang high-tech center, and centralized in the center its sourcing activities in China across all the industrial, health care, and infrastructure businesses it has here. The intent has been to cross-pollinate buying practices, look for ways to consolidate vendors and purchasing across the businesses, and leverage centralized resources to boost China sourcing across the board.

Today, GE has shifted much of its decision-making responsibilities regarding sourcing to China, greatly improving its ability to make sourcing decisions quickly. With over six hundred full-time sourcing employees now in Zhangjiang, GE has in place essentially a full complement of sourcing capabilities, from supplier development to product qualification and logistics control. Local R&D staff is housed in the center as well, to coordinate with supply managers. Most of the tools and practices common in GE's sourcing activities in established markets are now in use in China, including sophisticated supplier development programs such as launching lean Six Sigma projects to help improve supplier capabilities, and providing leadership training to executives at key supplier companies.

IBM has also raised the bar significantly on its sourcing aspirations in China. In 2006, IBM moved its global procurement headquarters to Shenzhen—the first time an IBM enterprise function has ever been located outside the United States. At the time of the move, IBM already had over eighteen hundred procurement employees in China, and was sourcing about one-third of its US$45 billion annual procurement spending from suppliers in Asia.

The Asia supply line is the carotid artery of IBM's industry, and IBM has been cultivating suppliers in China since the mid-1990s. The company did not change its sourcing strategy—it maintains procurement staff in sixty nations to stay close to customers and suppliers. But IBM's senior executives moved the company's procurement headquarters to China in recognition of the relatively powerful role that Asian suppliers and Chinese markets will play in IBM's future. It moved decision-making power to China because it has to get this right: IBM must develop a larger pool of low-cost suppliers to support the business not only in Asia but also globally. (IBM is planning for sales growth in China—and Asia generally—and wants a reliable supply base to feed that growth, but is actively seeking to leverage low-cost China-based supply to feed margin growth globally.) Moreover, the company eventually hopes that their Shenzhen operations—working collaboratively with suppliers—will become a hub for emerging new products and services for global customers.

Competitive Advantage

The impact that China sourcing can have for a global company's bottom line is significant. Over the longer term there are even greater advantages—competitive advantages—to be gained by setting (and achieving) high aspirations for sourcing in China for global as well as local markets. A few multinational sourcing executives in China who see these broader strategic opportunities are working with their corporate peers to coax forward organizational changes that will make near-term and longer-term gains possible. For instance, a few companies intend to shift design approval and ordering decisions from corporate offices in the home country to China. They also would like to integrate design and manufacturing functions and co-locate them in China.

These broader organizational changes won't happen overnight. But when they do happen, we think the impact could be enormous. Companies that get it right will be in a position to establish a long-term source of competitive advantage by taking the operations they build in China today to the next level.

One way would be to cut cycle times. By locating sample and specification approvals in China for products in industries ranging from casting to machined parts to clothing to consumer electronics, the turnaround time for getting a product or component into mass production can be dramatically shortened. Pushing this further and allowing the China office to handle prototype approval and final product ordering would add even more value. Currently, most procurement offices in China still rely on headquarters for these decisions. This requires the movement back and forth of samples or people, adding significant time and expense to the product development and ordering cycle. By moving decision making to China and keeping it close to the manufacturing operations of suppliers, companies could trim by one-third to one-half the time needed to develop and make new products.

Bringing China-made products to market more quickly would have a radical impact on a company's economics by improving its understanding of consumers, increasing the accuracy of forecasts, and reducing stockouts and markdowns. European "fast-fashion" retailers such as H&M and Zara have shown the possibilities of this model, though working with suppliers a little closer to home in eastern Europe.

The MNC executives we've talked with who are considering these moves do not underestimate the difficulties involved. We frequently hear executives in China say that the hardest part of sourcing in China is headquarters. Aspirations to increase China sourcing frequently are undermined in the home office by middle managers who believe they are acting in their function's best interests but actually are impeding the interests of the company overall. Supply managers measured in inventory turns, for example, might worry that distant and uncertain supply lines will require them to hold larger inventories, thereby driving up costs and reducing turns. Similarly, logistics managers, who are evaluated on their ability to economize, warn that far-flung suppliers will push up costs. Procurement managers at home wave yellow flags about the quality of goods, and product designers, manufacturing chiefs, and plant managers all have objections of their own.

Companies such as GE have managed to break through organizational resistance to sourcing by sending an unambiguous message from the top that China sourcing is a corporate goal. Business unit heads and the CEOs of GE's China operations are all held accountable for boosting sourcing from China. Additionally, GE decentralized control over supplier selection so that these decisions are made jointly by function managers from sourcing, technology, quality control, and finance.

One manufacturing company helped its managers at home to "get over it" by using its existing processes to select, approve, negotiate with, and manage new Chinese suppliers, instead of setting up a special initiative staffed by employees whose powers usurped the authority of current sourcing and product managers. Processes and sourcing roles changed only after the company became comfortable working with Chinese suppliers. Executives at this manufacturing company believe the experiment helped its managers design a better overall China sourcing program with clear decision rights and processes by allowing managers to gradually learn new approaches, build trust, and more comfortably buy in to ever-increasing China sourcing targets.

Headquarters isn't the only hurdle to cross, however. Increasing procurement requires the company to build a staff of people in China capable of making the right decisions for the company. Talented engineers and designers must be moved from headquarters—whether New York, Milwaukee, Paris, or Dusseldorf—or recruited and trained on the ground in China. GE hired local sourcing talent in China, then rotated these new employees into headquarters to help them learn advanced sourcing skills and attend management development training programs. Today most of the company's midlevel management appointments at the China center are promotions of talented staff who have put to good use in China what they learned in the head office. A German home products company, on the other hand, hired experienced Chinese staff and then brought over engineers from Germany—some temporarily, some permanently—to work with them.

Sourcing in China complicates product development decision making when these functions are half a world apart. A few MNCs are planning to integrate design and manufacturing functions and co-locate them in China to reduce design-to-order cycle times. Executives at these MNCs have taken to heart lessons from the notebook computer industry, which has blazed this trail to good effect. In that sector, original-design manufacturers (ODMs) from Taiwan, such as Compal Electronics and Quanta Computer, have emerged as leading players, with in-house design teams working side by side with those that oversee the manufacturing process. Notebook computer players that took this path typically saw overall costs drop between 10 and 15 percent because the teams could be staffed with Asia-based industrial designers and because the teams were able to better design products to cost and to solve manufacturing challenges more quickly. One mobile phone handset maker that took this approach in an established market reduced its design-to-order cycle time by 35 percent. It could work for companies in China, too.

This strategy should be possible for a wide range of products, making it of particular interest to retailers. "China sourcing must be managed from China—not from the U.S., and not even from Hong Kong buying offices, which are too far from the Chinese factories and the information they need," says Diane Long, head of adidas's China sourcing.[2] Long has been sourcing in China for twenty years. Before joining adidas, she was head of the Shanghai-based sourcing office of Liz Claiborne, and cochaired the sourcing committee of the U.S. Chamber of Commerce in Shanghai. Based on her experience here, she argues that companies in the apparel industry should strive to get designers to spend more time in Asia—or even move to Asia.

"Having design here, or operating transnationally [six months in China, and six in New York], would have several benefits,"

Long says. "The first is in inspiration—a lot of global trends start on the streets and in the factories of Asia. Second is around cost, and not just the salaries of the designers. Let me give you an example. If a designer is here, they will be more likely to pick a material or an accessory that is here in China and that the vendor already has." In the apparel sector, there are frequent tales of designers in New York or Paris who pick a button or a ribbon from a Japanese vendor that is two or three times (sometimes even five to ten times) more costly than a comparable product of equal quality from a local vendor. Buying from the Japanese vendor also adds six weeks for delivery of the product to the Chinese factory where the dress, blouse, or jacket will be assembled. "Having people who set the product specifications here on the ground makes a big difference," Long says.

"The third benefit of having designers in China," she continues, "is time. In apparel, higher-end garments designed and made in China can take thirty-six to forty-two weeks to get from concept to store, down from about a year. Some of the time saved is through better sourcing, like buying fabric in China instead of importing it, but having designers there can shorten lead times by at least 30 percent. Having designers here shortens the product development cycle. If they are here, they can approve samples faster, and work with factories more efficiently. These are changes in our sector that would have been unthinkable a few years back, but are very much on the table in China now."

Chinese suppliers with strong R&D capacities are emerging for almost all household goods, with early signs that apparel suppliers such as Li & Fung and Luen Tai are following suit. Retailers would be wise to continue to develop relationships with these suppliers and with those product OEMs with design and manufacturing units already in place in China. Technology companies have done it; other industries can follow.

Executives in other sectors operating in China are looking beyond cost-per-unit advantages to more strategic ones. In the high-tech sector, for instance, companies that have strong ties to suppliers in China—such as the ties IBM is hoping to develop with some of its suppliers in Asia, and companies such as Dell and Hewlett-Packard already have—could begin to instill global best practices into their supply chains there, further reducing operating costs and improving lead times. Toyota, for instance, is establishing the same kind of relationships and structures with its suppliers in China as it has with suppliers in Japan and North America.

Other manufacturers are looking at how to set up performance management structures that would reward innovation or share the benefits of cost reductions. "We are beginning to see a new wave of Chinese vendors who are anticipating the market and coming to us with innovations," says Diane Long. "There is a vendor in Jiangsu who is seeking a few smaller European brands so that his technicians will gain exposure to their more advanced fashion concepts. He hopes that will in turn allow his team to offer richer ideas to other customers. This market is really changing."

Adapting Global Standards

The strategies discussed earlier are all proven best practices that MNCs and their suppliers are familiar with elsewhere in the world. But companies need to commit to bold achievements and then put some muscle into adapting global standards to their procurement and supply operations in China. So far this chapter has focused largely on how companies should set higher aspirations for sourcing from China for their global operations. But let's bring it back to China.

For companies to crack new markets with new products in China, they need to get their procurement and sourcing operations into world-class shape. For products made in China for Chinese markets, companies need to reduce supply and procurement costs and to strengthen ties with suppliers to improve delivery and quality today and broaden their value chain and flexibility tomorrow. They also need better ties with vendors to foster innovation. All this additionally serves the MNC's global plans, as we've discussed, but (aside from fixing the disconnect with headquarters) getting sourcing into shape starts here.

Multinational companies in China need to do a lot of work to boost the capabilities of suppliers. To improve their own manufacturing productivity in China—to do lean right—they need to bring suppliers up to global standards. For instance, Chinese suppliers' component failure rates are higher than global standards, their deliveries are not sufficiently reliable, and their costs could be squeezed through more attention to efficiency and reduction of waste. (Rejected parts of incoming components run as high as 7 percent in some industries; 1 percent is the norm in established supply chains in developed markets.) Procurement and supply management practices that companies have honed to a fine groove in developed markets work well in China, too—with some adaptation—to meet these challenges.

Western supply management techniques now being introduced by MNC manufacturers in China include measuring suppliers' performance with objective scorecards, which help suppliers understand what is expected of them and form the basis for dialogue regarding performance. Suppliers become clearer on what they need to do to stay in good standing or even to increase their share of a customer's volume—or whether they are at risk of being cut off.

GE, P&G, and other companies have adapted their supplier audit processes, a fairly standardized procedure with developed suppliers in the United States, to the realities of working with suppliers in China. In the United States, auditors run through a checklist with suppliers, conducting it as an interview. In China, suppliers that are certified to meet standards (such as ISO standards) don't always consistently produce to those standards, so auditors have done spot checks on production lines, watching as parts are made. GE has also introduced its global online reverse auction system to suppliers in China. The online bidding system allows for real-time competitive bidding by suppliers for orders. In the United States, the system is quite complex, reflecting the sophistication that has come into these systems over time. In China, GE built a simplified version, translated the system into Chinese, and taught suppliers how to log on to the Internet and access the reverse auction system.

Carrefour has also introduced an online bidding and reverse auction system in China. The retailer has also become a design-to-cost evangelist. Carrefour has sent engineers into the development operations of select high-volume suppliers to train them on design-to-cost principles and practices. Other proven global best practices in supply management that Carrefour has introduced to its supply chain in China include building and managing warehouses in large Chinese cities to split and consolidate orders, sharing demand information in China with one hundred fifty of its strategic Chinese suppliers, and even linking information about global demand with its China supply chain.

The giant retailer has actively adapted a number of proven procurement practices in China. It has a good reason to do so. In Carrefour's ninety-nine stores throughout China (as of June 2007), 95 percent of the commodities sitting on miles of shelf space come from local suppliers. (That does not include the goods that Carrefour sources in China and sells through its stores elsewhere in the world.) For instance, Carrefour purchased US$4.6 billion in goods from more than fourteen hundred Chinese suppliers in 2005. Today, China is one of the most important hubs in Carrefour's global supply base, with over two hundred employees in its sourcing operations in Shanghai alone. (The company also has eleven procurement offices in different cities throughout the Yangtze Delta region to be close to key customer electronics and textile suppliers.) Through its commitment to China sourcing, Carrefour has won favor from a number of local governments.

The retailer established specialized purchasing groups within its operations, just as Carrefour—and many other companies—does elsewhere in the world. This helps the retailer increase purchasing efficiency, as it would anywhere. Companies such as Carrefour have to do very little tailoring to implement the approach in China—they just have to do it.

Companies are adopting other proven procurement tools and approaches to improve their purchasing capabilities. Procurement managers in China recognize that they have to better understand suppliers' costs in order to negotiate the right price for parts and supplies. As mentioned previously, the cost competitiveness of Chinese companies comes not only from labor on the assembly line but also from lower R&D and management costs as well as lower-cost capital equipment. Procurement managers need to understand where the value is.

Clean-sheet costing is a well-known technique that procurement managers in North America and Europe use to negotiate with suppliers to drive down the current price and, more important, set targets for future cost improvements that can be shared with the supplier. Understanding the economics of your suppliers creates transparency that initiates a fact-based dialogue with suppliers rather than price haggling. It is a tool that can be used in China without any local tweaking. For instance, we recently helped one technology company in China develop a clean-sheet analysis of its PC board suppliers' costs. The technology company's managers shared the analysis with their suppliers. In the ensuing discussion, we found that we had overestimated some costs and underestimated others, but not by a lot. The discussion focused on costs and margins, and led suppliers to offer the technology company a 20 percent price reduction in supply in return for consolidating some buying.

Linear performance pricing is another common procurement technique that works well in China. It is an analysis that builds on comparing price to performance rather than on a supplier's intrinsic economics. The chosen performance factor of the various products on the market is plotted against their price. If the supplier's price falls high above the revealed trend line, negotiation can ensue on why that gap exists and the possible ways to reduce it. If other products fall well below the trend line, they may be studied for production or supply innovations that allow their lower price. The technique is also ready-made to negotiate future price points when the supplier is able to lift its product to a higher performance level.

Execution Is in the Details

Finally, sourcing well in China is about paying attention to the details. Sourcing is essentially a complicated set of activities involving many detailed decisions, from selecting suppliers to managing production, quality, inventory, and logistics. Executives know that companies can stumble in any of these activities as they expand their sourcing options around the world. What surprises executives about sourcing in China is the number of details that can go wrong and the effort required to hold a program together. Companies find that they have to pay much more attention than expected to monitoring their suppliers' processes—working back from expected delivery dates to check that suppliers receive raw materials on time and meet every subsequent milestone until the products ship.

Without hands-on supervision and quick action when milestones are missed, companies face delays. Intensive monitoring is required in every industry and with most suppliers in China. This level of attention, though not unheard of elsewhere, is far more prevalent in China than other countries. Companies that haven't mastered the details incur shipment delays and additional costs. More important, some find that because they are constantly fighting fires, it is difficult to scale up the sourcing they do in China.

Diane Long advises American Chamber of Commerce members in China to pay "unrelenting attention to detail." It is one of the factors that separates good-enough from world-class sourcing practice here. "Understand the exact process used to make the product, from beginning to end, and never be satisfied that it will be done well without watching every step. Do not accept general explanations. And do not accept *meiyou wen ti* (no problem) as an answer, because when a vendor in China says *meiyou wen ti*, you can count on there being a small problem that is growing into a big one! If a mistake happens, it is usually because someone failed to follow the disciplined process that has been mapped out for them. We use a 'five whys' dialogue to find out what went wrong—literally asking 'Why?' five times until you get to the bottom of it."

Language barriers do occasionally get in the way of this work. For instance, Long recalled accompanying a U.S. congresswoman on a factory visit in China. (For a time, Long cochaired the sourcing committee of the American Chamber of Commerce in Shanghai.) Long speaks fluent Mandarin, and listened as the congresswoman asked questions through an interpreter. "She asked if the

Chinese government does anything to encourage exports. The interpreter translated it verbatim and the factory owner answered 'no,' which was an accurate answer of the literal question. But the spirit of the question did not come through. So I asked some follow-up questions to go deeper. 'Do you get a VAT rebate when you export?' The reply was yes. 'Does the Investment Commission visit you and help you?' Again, yes—they helped with loans and other support, the factory owner said. So in the end the factory owner recognized that, in many ways, he *does* get government support. I have found the same thing happens in business questions." Questions are asked and answered in good faith, but meanings are a world apart.

Sourcing in China is already big, but much bigger days are ahead. For MNCs, there is urgent need to build real procurement capabilities in China, particularly in setting higher sourcing aspirations, overcoming the organizational barriers that are getting in the way of achieving more, and adapting global standard sourcing practices and tools to source more goods at better prices. Distributing the products that ultimately result from this sourcing presents its own set of challenges, as discussed in the following chapter.

CHAPTER SEVEN

Distribution:
Changing Times

Getting products to new markets in China efficiently and cost-effectively is probably the most perplexing challenge multinational companies face as they expand from the big eastern cities into wider circles of smaller-tier cities. Constraints are numerous—from legal to logistical—but getting the right distribution and sales operating model in place will be a critical determinant of success.

To understand just how critical it is, consider how distribution models played a role with serious competitive stakes in the mobile telephone sector a few years ago. China has become the world's largest market for mobile telephones, with more than 90 million cell phones sold in China during 2005 alone, and unit sales breaking the 100 million mark in 2006. It is also one of the world's most competitive markets. Here, global giants such as Nokia, Samsung, and Sony Ericsson—all of which view China as a critical market—battle for sales against each other and against domestic handset manufacturers such as Lenovo, TCL, Ningbo Bird, Konka, and others. The multinational companies have long had a much larger share of market than the domestic companies in China—and Nokia is overall market leader—but earlier this decade the domestic companies rose from nowhere to provisionally pose a threat to the multinational giants, largely due to how they managed their channels and got products into the hands of customers. The giants beat back the upstarts in a number of ways, including adopting—with adaptations—the distribution strategies pioneered by the domestic companies.

When Nokia, Sony Ericsson, and other international handset makers first started to sell mobile phones in China, during the 1990s, they established channel and distribution models reflecting the realities of operating in China at that time: the government tightly regulated distribution and logistics (and still does), forcing MNCs to work within the confines of a distribution structure that dated to the days of a planned economy.[1] Under these constraints, MNCs appointed national distributors and worked through layers of regional and local distributors. There were variations in the approaches each took, of course, but broadly speaking, the models they adopted were shaped by regulation. Nokia, for instance, entered China in 1985, and by 2003 the network feeding Nokia handsets to Chinese customers included three national distributors, twenty provincial distributors, and more than fifteen hundred individual dealers to reach the ten thousand or more sales points. Nokia's network was emblematic of distribution arrangements established by many MNCs. With layers of distributors to work through, and a heavy reliance on point-

of-sale promotions to influence customer experience at retail outlets, the MNC model was a recipe for brand dilution. The quality
of customer experience through these touchpoints was frequently poor.

Domestic competitors to Nokia built a different distribution
model that proved quickly to be much more effective. Ningbo
Bird, for instance, had by 2000 a network in third- and fourth-
tier cities that included selling through twenty-eight provincial
sales companies, three hundred sales offices, fifteen thousand
local distributors, and over fifty thousand retail outlets, and had
five thousand salespeople to work with retailers and interact directly with customers.

Initially Bird had tried to get a foothold in the handset market
by accessing one of the MNC's established distribution networks.
The company tried to negotiate an agreement with established
distributors, but was rebuffed by distributors and dealers that
chose to remain loyal to their MNC partners. In response, Bird,
TCL, and others sought a different route to customers. (The domestic companies were not as constrained by the distribution
regulations that have hampered foreign companies; some of these
regulations were relaxed in 2004 for companies in many sectors,
but other restrictions remain.)[2] Reaching customers directly
through retailers, and through hundreds of thousands of salespeople and in-store promoters, the domestic companies had far
greater control over their prices and the experience they provided customers. Also, they could get direct customer feedback
to gain better insights into emerging consumer trends.

Bird and TCL started taking share away from the MNCs during 2002 and 2003. But the domestic companies' brief and heady
rise wouldn't last more than a year. As of 2006, Nokia had an estimated 30 percent share of the market, according to most analysts, while the top domestic competitor—Lenovo—had just 6

percent, and other domestic rivals much less. This is a tough and volatile sector in China, and you have to execute many things well to succeed. Distribution is one of those things—a point not lost on Nokia. The global mobile phone company has since transformed its distribution model, taking lessons learned from the provisional successes Bird and TCL scored, and building on them. For instance, Nokia has been rationalizing distribution layers and broadening its retail reach. Today it has over five thousand salespeople selling directly to retailers. Nokia executives have publicly stated that their new distribution strategy played a significant role in boosting the company's performance in China.

Distribution is critical to success in China, and success in distribution requires an ability to learn and adapt. Operating one's own retail network is by no means the right distribution model for every sector in China today. But being proactive in continually adopting better ways to get products into the hands of customers is most assuredly a capability that MNCs in every sector should develop. The "right" model is a moving target. Nokia and other MNC companies adopted the right distribution approaches at the time they entered the market. But they were caught by surprise when domestic rivals exploited opportunities for switching to more efficient ones. The lesson for MNCs in other industries in China is that as competition in other sectors becomes as intense as it is in mobile phones, clinging to outmoded models of distribution even for just two to three years can be very costly.

To improve their execution in managing channels and distributing goods in China, MNCs have to do more than adapt good global practices. Certainly there are good standards and practices that work well in more mature markets and can serve as models here—good account management practices, for instance, and approaches for identifying and smoothing out channel conflicts. With some tweaking, they work in China, too, as we describe later in this chapter. But identifying and adapting superlative distribution and sales practices will be a volatile game for some time because so much of what governs success in distribution is in flux—such as government regulations and immature distribution structures—and because what it takes to be successful in getting products to customers in China's heartlands isn't clear yet. Under these circumstances, experimentation and learning are as critical to good execution as adapting global standards to a China context.

China's distribution structure is between two worlds: an old one that is not yet behind us and a new one that is not yet here. In the old world of the planned economy, distributors had power, and everyone who worked through them had to comply with their wishes. The core assumption of allocation and distribution in a planned economy was that goods were scarce. The state-owned distribution system moved goods from producers to consumers via processes that made sense to the distribution system, not to stakeholders at either end of the system.

Today, the market economy has tilted China toward plenty, not scarcity; oversupply in nearly every category stands at one end of the distribution system, and a mushrooming base of buyers at the other. In the middle, distributors are now more often private enterprises than state-owned ones, but operate as little more than order fillers for producers, providing very little value when compared with distributors in developed economies. Distributors in every sector are narrowly focused, and the network as a whole is highly fragmented. This, too, is a legacy of a distribution system rooted in a planned economy. Whereas once distributors were local bureaus affiliated with the state-owned system, today they are enterprises that have expanded little beyond their inherited connections. In most sectors, distributors today focus on one particular city. Only a few have a regional reach. National reach? Maybe someday, but not today.

Distribution in the automotive sector provides an example that speaks for many other industries. There are over twenty-five hundred registered automotive dealers in Beijing alone today. Only one hundred of these dealers have annual sales of more than two hundred cars. Most of the rest are nonexclusive yards, with limited after-sales service capabilities and weak financial capabilities. "Retailing" for most is a parking lot where dusty cars lie waiting for prospective buyers. Brand management, marketing, and customer relationship management simply do not exist. In construction equipment, the situation is even worse. Global construction equipment companies such as Komatsu must cope with thousands of "traders," some of whom are simply one-man shops peddling their personal relationships in exchange for kickbacks.

Logistics is also caught between an old world and a new one. China has invested rapidly and massively to improve the highway infrastructure in many provinces over the past twenty years, yet logistics costs remain high. On average, China's relative distribution costs—still highly dependent on trucking—are two and a third times higher than in the United States. Trucking is not cheap and does not run smoothly. Expensive special licenses are needed for trucks to cross provincial borders (to avoid having to unload and reload to a local truck), access to city centers is limited to off-peak times, and road tolls are comparatively high. Information systems are still immature, hampering the easy transfer of information between customers and suppliers and driving up the cost of warehousing and in-transit inventory. In electronics industries, China averages fifty-one inventory days, compared with eight days in the United States. At the same time, distributors lack automated or integrated tracking systems, so that drawing information from multiple manual and computerized systems to trace and ensure delivery is a time-consuming and expensive process.

These transportation and information problems will improve, and logistics costs will go down—probably rapidly over the next decade—but for now, MNCs must factor in costs and regulatory challenges to their channel plans. At the same time, their channel plans for broadening distribution from premier markets in first- and second-tier cities to premium and middle markets in third- and fourth-tier cities are fraught with uncertainty. (MNCs that offer business products and services, whether photocopiers or construction equipment, are also spreading out around the country, chasing a usually high number of small to medium-sized enterprises and self-employed entrepreneurs.) Particularly knotty is the problem of reconciling coverage with quality in a cost-effective manner. The answer to these questions will emerge and best practices will become clear—but we aren't there yet. In the meantime, experimentation, learning, and adaptation are the hallmarks of successful execution.

Creative Approaches to Distribution

Multinational executives in China should post a sign with the single word "Innovate" in the offices of their distribution managers. China's old stratified distribution system can sabotage any effort greater than a dabble. The loss of brand message, service, and control through each layer is significant, and there are more layers in China than in most countries. Companies such as Samsung, Fuji Xerox, P&G, and others have boldly experimented with new approaches to covering their markets. Most important, they set a direction but then continue to adapt—and to build new insights, skills, and capabilities.

Based on the successes we've seen these MNCs achieve, we've identified four approaches they are taking to distribution. Each is a creative approach to distribution, given the realities and constraints of getting goods to customers in China today. Each is a flexible approach, allowing for change, rather than involving more rigid structures. And each approach is a vehicle for experimenting and learning in an environment of flux.

Pursue Hybrid Channel Schemes

Accessing consumers or business customers in China's dispersed lower-tier areas is extremely difficult. The low volume of purchasing that most MNCs are currently seeing in these areas limits how much service support companies can provide and the degree to which they can control the quality of customer experiences. These are markets to build, and building them requires a more hands-on approach than the typical multitiered distribution structure that most MNCs have in place today.

Best practice in distribution is to try to get as close to your customer as you can. In China, that isn't very close. Markets are so fragmented, dispersed, and immature that it is simply too expensive and impractical to try to replicate state-of-the art sales models found in Europe and the United States. Instead, some innovative companies have developed hybrid structures using a combination of existing distributors and a direct sales force. Alternatively, they may choose to put distributor representatives on the company payroll. In other words, they partner with the distributor or integrate the distributor to get a step or two closer to customers than they otherwise might.

With premium products, a company may be able to set up parallel networks to ensure that customers receive the service and quality they pay for. This is essentially the model that Bird and TCL pioneered. They leveraged distributors in select regions, but in most regions built a sales force to deal with retailers directly. This approach allowed Bird and TCL to rapidly penetrate second- to fourth-tier cities.

Hybrid distribution or sales approaches aren't unique to China, of course. What's unique is the need to continually adjust the balance—compress one channel and expand another—as conditions change, or even to be successful in different cities. Procter & Gamble provides one example of just how dynamic a company must be. In 1989, P&G sold product through the limited sales force and customer network of its partner, Guangzhou Soap. Over the next three years, P&G gained access through its partner to one hundred fifty wholesale outlets. The wholesalers shipped products to retail stores and collected money, but did not provide store coverage or in-store merchandising services.

By 1992, however, P&G's total receivables in China surpassed 100 million renminbi, or seventy days' sales. It was time to evolve. P&G cut off accounts that were more than forty-five days due, and started to recruit a sales force. Over the next two years, P&G replaced its partner's sales force with its own to cover stores, groceries, and kiosks in its top forty first- and second-tier city markets. The sales force worked on pricing and shelf placement, as well as introducing P&G's expanding line of products. As the company built relationships with key retailers, P&G's remaining wholesale distributors became more active in developing customers and more adept at store coverage and sales fundamentals, thereby further driving sales.

As P&G began to expand into hundreds of additional cities during the mid-1990s, it put in systems to manage inventory, sales processes, and customer information. The information provided by the system helped lift distributors' management skills and further locked them in to P&G's business. By the late 1990s, local and global competitors began to put pressure on P&G's

relatively high cost structure. In response, P&G decided to increase localization of brands, expand into low-price products, and aggressively streamline overhead costs. In concert with these moves, P&G switched from a regional sales structure to a channel-based one. In 1997, the company cut the number of its distributors from three hundred fifty to one hundred fifty, established key account teams (with their own finance and logistics experts), and directed marketing teams to specialize along trade, customer, and category lines. As the number of distributors fell and specialists' skills rose, the margins of key distributors and their relationships with the larger retail chains in China improved markedly. P&G products gained better in-store positioning than the wares of competitors.

In recent years, P&G has expanded its presence in China's countryside—the heartland. Through each of these channel and distribution evolutions—five in just fifteen years—sales continued to soar.

Another company that has successfully adopted a hybrid model is Xian Janssen Pharmaceutical, a joint venture company formed by Johnson & Johnson and one of the most successful foreign pharmaceutical companies in China. Xian Janssen came to the hybrid model the other way around, however. During the 1990s, Xian Janssen bypassed the first-tier state-owned distribution companies in its sector and built a direct sales force focused on selling to doctors and hospitals in select, large urban markets. By 2002, however, domestic competitors were stealing market share in several of Janssen's product areas by selling to retail drugstores and private clinics in lower-tier cities. Janssen systematically reviewed its position at each level of the market—by product, segment, and region—and concluded that it needed to work with distributors, particularly to carry product to rural areas. It selected distributors based on their willingness to hire staff and dedicate them to Janssen, and gave the distributors geographic exclusivity in the rural areas. Then it invested in training the distributors' staff in sales and marketing techniques, even though they were on the distributors' payrolls. The channel makeover paid off: today Janssen remains the market leader, particularly in fast-growing rural areas, having stemmed any further erosion to its market share while it avoided the potentially ruinous cost of extending its sales force into what were marginal sales areas.

Consider Alternative Partners

In many developed global markets, MNCs have been refining their distribution models for decades. They have often built deep expertise into their distribution arrangements by tracing and serving the global supply chains. Newcomers do not easily overtake the established players in these markets. But in China—the world's factory—distribution companies are well short of world class and have not yet become established and dominant players in their respective sectors. Thus, while the market is relatively underdeveloped, there are many companies with the cash and skill, acquired either in China or elsewhere, to build a better solution. You may have to think creatively about where to find them, however.

Companies can look for distribution partners that may be outside their industry altogether. What's important is that the partner demonstrates a capacity to learn and develop skills, or has an asset that you can leverage. The prospective partner might not be an obvious choice from a developed market perspective, but it has the intrinsics to develop the kind of distribution skills you need to get into the markets you want to be in. Be prepared to think out of the box when assessing options.

Samsung pursued this approach. When Samsung came to China in 2001, it faced strong competition from Hewlett-Packard and Epson, which had built their positions in the printer market through strong relationships with leading Chinese information technology (IT) distributors. At the time, seven primary IT distributors handled over 70 percent of laser printer sales, and all proved to be biased in their efforts toward the incumbent brands. For example, Epson relied on five of these distributors to see its machines through a network of four hundred forty secondary distributors and over three thousand dealers. Only one hundred eighty of these dealers were exclusive—with the rest, Epson was competing for sales side by side with all other brands.

Unable to secure a distribution relationship with any of the top seven local distributors, Samsung worked with an unexpected ally. Samsung appointed a well-financed auto parts dealer as its exclusive national partner and sole agent (the partner was looking to make better use of its distribution chain). Though the partner had no prior IT product distribution experience, it had the financial resources and entrepreneurial will to build a strong one. Samsung introduced price controls as well as dealer monitoring and financing, but also offered the partner generous terms to push Samsung printers.

Samsung didn't just stop with negotiating the right terms with its partner. The two then established a "closed club" system, in which Samsung took on only two dealers as agents in each Chinese district, and used a number of tactics to ensure stable retail prices and protect the channel economics for each member of the distribution partnership. Within two years of its China launch, Samsung had risen to number three in the market, attaining an 11.2 percent share.

Complement Distributors with Critical Capabilities

In developed markets, distributors provide three basic functions: representation, finance, and logistics. In the constrained environment in China, the brand owner may have to undertake much of the heavy lifting in each of these three areas for now. Distributors lack much of the product and market knowledge needed to do an effective job of, for instance, in-store selling or after-sales service. Although influential local distributors might gain bank financing to support a specific customer sale, few have the financial wherewithal or the knowledge to put together more significant deals themselves. Increasingly, MNCs (or their big Chinese rivals) are providing services lacking in China's distribution channels.

Haier, China's leading consumer appliance company, built its own after-sales service network beginning in the late 1990s to compete with multinational and Chinese rivals. The traditional approach—the one Haier's competitors took—was to rely on third-party technicians to deliver after-sales service. Haier's customers can call a toll-free hotline (one of the first in China) with service requests. Within twenty-four hours a polite, uniformed man will show up at the door, with all the necessary parts and tools, a towel on which to lay them out, and the mission of fixing the problem and cleaning up afterward. A follow-up call the next day to check on service quality completes the transaction. Not surprisingly, Chinese consumers now say that Haier sets the benchmark for after-sales service, not just in consumer electronics but in anything from mobile phones to cars.

Riding on the wave of consumer demand for premium after-sales service, Haier now charges a price premium in the white goods market that is even higher than that of some of the multinational brands. Providing this level of service in China is expensive: cheap labor counts for little here, because such service requires distribution centers, retail outlets, a fleet of trucks to deliver parts, and sophisticated IT systems. The investment for Haier paid off because after-sales service proved to be a competitive advantage in its sector. The point of this example, however, is that opportunities exist for companies to offer more than what the current distribution chain offers.

Financing is another area of opportunity. The law currently prevents MNCs such as Caterpillar from offering vendor financing to prospective customers. Following the surge in bad debts in the late 1990s, however, China's banks have become unwilling to lend to private or collectively owned companies to buy machinery. Caterpillar found a creative solution. The company leveraged its good relations with local dealers—and *their* local banks—to assist some customers to secure financing themselves. The big equipment maker also pressed the government for a business license to provide lease financing. (Caterpillar and GE Capital are, as of this writing, the only foreign companies to hold such a license.) To obtain the license, Caterpillar successfully made the case that its ability to finance equipment purchases would help China's state-owned enterprises overcome their own capital constraints, because loans from the government were being limited to the top one or two hundred state enterprises.

Caterpillar was not alone in pursuing finance solutions to complement the distribution chain of its sector. Hyundai and Daewoo introduced delayed payment terms for purchases of their construction equipment, rapidly gaining market share. GE and Siemens both saw the need for vendor financing to enable prospective purchasers to meet the prices for infrastructure goods, although they responded to the need in different ways. GE, supported as always by GE Capital, was able to provide that financing directly. Siemens prevailed upon the German government to offer loans to Chinese purchasers on attractive terms. Siemens has become the leading supplier of rail cars and electrical systems for railways in China, and GE comfortably leads the aircraft engine market.

We should note that although customer financing is an option that MNCs in other sectors might want to pursue, it is a path studded with risks. China lacks databases on credit histories, for instance, so financing consumer items won't work—item costs won't adequately cover the credit risks. Banks used to offer companies insurance against customer default, but that made lending too easy and contributed to the enormous pile of consumer bad debts—reaching over US$13 billion by 2003—which put an end to such practices. Where credit is available in China today, consumers have to offer up to twenty references to receive the loan. Car financing may be an option, and multinational firms have been allowed to offer it since 2004. But they should think twice. The best strategy would be to work with a bank or other partner to leverage their skills and data and share the risk.

Adopt a Partnership Mind-set

Working in partnership with distributors has become global best practice. In China, that means MNCs sometimes need to be the kind of partners that share the wealth. Making partnerships work may require an MNC to think carefully about the economics of distributors or partners, and to make adjustments to make the economics work for everyone. Foreign companies that make and sell brands in China, for instance, want to ensure that domestic retailers are up to the job as partners in providing to customers. Domestic retailers have to offer high-quality customer service, but they also need to do a better job of collecting customer feedback, build better logistics systems, and develop more effective sales skills and more brand-conscious shop designs. Retailers need higher margins to pay for these improvements. At the same time, wholesalers increasingly find they must partially pay for goods when they take stock from producers (in the past they only paid when the retailer purchased the goods), help brand owners make retail coverage decisions, select retailers, manage stock and returns, and collect payments. They too must be compensated for their increasingly valuable role. If the economics do not work, no one competent will take on the job.

To build viable partnerships, MNCs sometimes have to help shape an environment for success for the Chinese partner. (As China's distribution sector works its way through revolutionary change, opportunities for shaping the development of distribution sectors abound—multinational companies could think of seizing these opportunities as ways of building for the future.) In the auto sector, for example, wholesalers are disappearing altogether as global brand owners increasingly turn to exclusive retailers. Honda and GM have both worked through the necessary economics to give their retailers the incentive to take on new investment and risks. The MNCs take into account the shared responsibilities of dealer training in retail management and customer service, as well as factor in regional cost structures as they expand their networks throughout China.

Sometimes partnership means being a coach and trainer. As P&G was actively redesigning its distribution structure every couple of years, it was also improving the skills of its partners. P&G set up a shadow management structure for distributors. Its own sales managers trained its local distributors in modern channel and inventory management skills and closely supervised their daily operations to ensure the quality of their channel coverage. This approach not only helped P&G build the best fast-moving consumer goods (FMCG) distribution system in China, achieving leadership in four of the seven product categories in which it competes, but also helped P&G cement its relationships with some of the best FMCG distributors, which is now a key competitive advantage.

Chinese distributors have been very open to such intervention, and keen to learn from the brand owner's ideas. You need to take some care, therefore, to guarantee that they do not use the same skills for your competitors. First, ensure that you represent a significant part of the distributor's business, so they won't risk loss of income by taking improper advantage of the training. Second, pay individual salespeople within the distributor a direct bonus based on their sales of your product. Then, build that loyalty further by certifying salespeople for their performance or skills level. Toyota, for example, treats its partner after-sales service technicians almost as employees, taking them through a certificate training program that will enable them to get jobs in Toyota dealerships or service agencies anywhere in China. These investments in loyalty do pay off, even though some good people will always move to the competitors. For evidence, companies such as Toyota track the turnover rates for their agencies, their customer service ratings and, ultimately, their market share.

The time is now for multinational companies in China to change their distribution stripes, but they'd better be prepared to keep changing them. In China, distribution and logistics capabilities are still emerging. Companies must be willing to experiment, learn, and adapt. They must also be able to recruit and develop talented employees, as discussed in chapter 8.

CHAPTER EIGHT

Talent Holds the Key

To raise the bar on execution in China—to become world class—the final piece of the puzzle is your people. To meet the needs of customers who want products with features that make sense to them and are sensitive to prices, and to compete with domestic rivals for those consumers, multinational companies must be good at utilizing what is fast becoming a scarce resource in China—talented employees. Companies are struggling now to recruit and develop top-flight local marketers, product designers, manufacturing and sourcing managers, distribution and sales personnel, and executive leaders. All signs indicate that the talent wars will only become more heated in the next few years, not less.

Fifteen years ago MNCs were willing to make compromises concerning the managers and staff they had in place in their operations in China because the opportunity was minor and because executives in headquarters bracketed China as something different—an unknown, an experiment. Besides, for important jobs, MNCs could send in an expatriate to oversee responsibilities. Today, the attitude is very different. Companies need employees who know and understand China and have a more nuanced understanding of how to win. Earlier in this decade, for instance, P&G sent many of its marketing and research expatriates home. Instead, the company staffed these positions with Chinese professionals who had international experience and were more familiar with local markets. And P&G isn't alone. Inside MNCs that are playing to win in China, there is growing recognition that having a balance of global and local staff for important positions is effective for achieving the kind of creative insights needed to make fast, competitive judgments.

Still, having a nuanced understanding of consumers and local costs is one thing—having experience and the necessary business and leadership skills to succeed inside a global organization is another. Expatriates here frequently come from the ranks of a company's best executives. But what about the skill base of local managers and staff? The answer, simply put, is that the pool of stars is growing, but not as fast as demand. Competition for the talented local people needed to grow a business is intense, and becomes more heated every day. Ten years ago, the executive team running an MNC's China operations typically reported to an Asia-Pacific unit. Now the team more typically reports to the company's U.S. or European headquarters. As a result, companies are seeking China leaders with the same skills and presence as their other regional leaders. Hundreds of foreign and multinational companies are pursuing such individuals right now, creating intense demand for a limited pool of talented, seasoned, global-company-style executives. Large domestic Chinese companies and fast-rising entrepreneurial ones are also competing to woo talented people. The demand isn't just for top teams. Multi-national companies are looking for talented functional managers and professionals, such as manufacturing or procurement managers or customer insight and branding directors. The heads of China sourcing offices, for example, are receiving package offers here that are well above those of their bosses back home, a fact reflecting market demand.

Chinese companies are fierce competitors to foreign companies in the talent wars because they can appeal to a talented manager's nationalistic pride and sense of mission. We've talked with many Chinese managers, born in China and frequently educated overseas, who told us they joined companies such as Haier, Lenovo, Baosteel, Ningbo Bird, Wanxiang, Chery, and others because they want to be part of the far-reaching effort to help Chinese companies compete globally. (Some of these companies are also hiring expatriates into key roles in a bid to gain the skills needed to compete with larger foreign companies with—on the whole—better skills.) Meanwhile, entrepreneurial companies are mushrooming here: talented Chinese and expatriate executives are jumping big-company ships to start new enterprises. Access to capital isn't difficult; friends and family frequently provide start-up funding, and start-up costs are significantly lower here than they are in Silicon Valley.

But MNCs can win more than their fair share of star recruits by playing their trump cards: experience, professionalism, and internationalism. Chinese executives generally view MNCs in China as better places to work than local ones. They reason that they can develop better skills and global executive experience at an international company. The training they can get in an MNC is more thorough and insightful, and the overall environment is more rewarding, with superior systems and processes. Multinational companies offer better benefits than even the best Chinese companies.

Additionally, Chinese executives see drawbacks to working in Chinese companies: the strong legacy of seniority-based systems at former state-owned enterprises makes it difficult for a star talent to find a position where he or she can have an impact, or see a clear development path.

Compensation is not the deciding issue for talented people in China. Compensation—particularly for executive and functional management—has been rising as companies compete for good people. Whereas an expatriate executive may cost a company US$500,000 (including housing, schooling for children, annual leave, and tax protection), a local executive of comparable ability now costs as much as US$300,000 or more. Multinational companies do tend to pay more than Chinese companies for executives and managers, but in our experience working across hundreds of multinational and domestic companies in China, the top priorities for stars are an ability to make decisions that matter to the company, career development, and learning (i.e., access to international standards, experiences, and skills). Compensation is a secondary consideration.

Compensation typically only becomes an issue for a candidate mulling over job options when autonomy and career development appear equivalent. Recently, a European company was able to hire an extremely talented Chinese sourcing executive, with no increase in compensation over his predecessor, because the company made it clear that in his new role the sourcing executive would enjoy greater influence and prospects for development. In fact, we believe that MNCs can fill their ranks with good people, who have the skills to execute, by providing these benefits while holding compensation to numbers that are fair market value. Of course, MNCs will still need to bid in the mid to high end of the range for the very best people available, as they do anywhere; however, if they carefully consider the key positions they need to fill with stars, they can create a good environment and keep compensation costs reasonable.

Similarly, escalating compensation isn't the lever to use to retain the talent you've won. Providing autonomy and development paths is not only a persuasive recruiting offer but also what motivates people to stay. An initial compensation offer has a very short shelf life in this market. But providing opportunities and experiences that people can't get elsewhere can frequently be a compelling counteroffer. Hewitt annually surveys top talent in China, and respondents tell Hewitt that their chief concerns include having exposure to senior management, career opportunities, development and education benefits, and housing benefits.

We can provide a more personal data point. Recently, an American-born Chinese executive (and good friend) who has been in China for many years was choosing between two competing job offers. He ultimately chose the offer that paid only 60 percent what the competing opportunity would have. Why? He had known the executive team members at the company he opted for longer, felt they were more committed to his career development, and saw this company as a longer-term opportunity for him.

This is where MNCs can excel in the talent wars. General Electric, Citigroup, HSBC, and others have fine-tuned leadership training and development programs in place globally; extending these to China has provided a competitive advantage in hiring and retaining top talent. These companies have clearly defined development tracks that begin when young people join the organization. They put most new employees in China on track to win potential leadership positions in their local operations, but they give high-potential employees a different treatment. Each company rotates star talent in positions inside China and in the company's operations outside China to prepare them to join the global management team. Each year HSBC, for example, puts four hundred handpicked international managers, including those from China, through a global-rotation program that trains them in world standards and practices. These apprenticeships and rotations help rising executives build internal global networks that allow for the transfer of knowledge, improved understanding of formal and informal processes, and greater trust. The managers also learn to distinguish the nonnegotiable aspects of the company's business model and processes from those they can adapt to China's needs. Senior leaders nurture and coach these talented managers and closely track their career development. (They also sometimes sweeten compensation.)

As a result, these companies attract and retain the best talent. Even though people leave to run other organizations—ex-Citigroup employees head banks across Asia, for instance—the companies' ability to regenerate this talent makes them very resilient. Their people stay long enough—five or six years rather than two or three—to feed insight back into that learning machine, to help replicate their own talent, and to ensure a strong and relatively stable executive team. In a market as dynamic as China's, that is some achievement.

Human Resource Systems for Growth

Leaders in talent management, such as HSBC and Siemens, have set the bar very high on how well they execute the core processes involved in recruiting, developing, motivating, and rewarding their managerial and professional staff. They expect their human resource (HR) standards and capabilities in China to be every bit as high as they are elsewhere in the world.

High standards for HR execution are rare among multinational companies in China. We would not say this is an area where companies excel. Yes, most MNCs have core processes in place for defining structured tiers of job grades, for linking compensation levels tied to job grades, and for externally benchmarking grade-level compensation to stay competitive. Yes, companies codify HR policies on such things as benefits, promotions, and mobility (transferring people to other locations) and communicate those policies to employees. Yes, they have defined recruiting practices and evaluation processes, and then reward performance. But we frequently see rudimentary shortcomings in one or more of these processes in most companies. Multinational companies in China simply aren't measuring up to their own global standards. But more important, we rarely find companies that have incorporated into their core processes mechanisms for truly nurturing talent in a China context.

Let's be clear about this. As mentioned in chapter 2, a critical principle for achieving world-class execution in China is to be tight on people, but loose on people control. By this we mean pay attention to nurturing, coaching, and developing people into capable managers, and be prepared to relax a bit on process instruction guides. You would nurture and coach in China as the best leaders do anywhere—by giving your people room to make their own assessments and use their own judgment, and letting them succeed and sometimes fail. They need to experiment, reflect, learn, and become seasoned. It makes no sense, then, to constrain people in narrowly defined processes or to micromanage their decision making. You don't want to grade your next-generation managers on how well they follow instructions; instead, you want them to learn how to lead and excel. Thus, the skill you're looking for in the talent you are nurturing is judgment. Good judgment. Shrewd judgment.

The HR systems and processes that are best practice in the world fit in China, too. Many companies built their HR systems ten years ago, reflecting their understanding of what they could or could not accomplish at the time. Regulations in China guided hiring, firing, compensation, and benefit rules. Cultural differences—such as the need for hierarchy—seemed to require unique approaches rather than modifications of existing global approaches.

But labor regulations have changed, and, in the end, the cultural differences don't require wholesale restructuring of global systems. They require thoughtful adaptation. Multinational companies that have put into place HR systems that vary widely from their global systems—and, frankly, that operate systems that are lax by comparison with global standards—need to make these systems measure up to global standards. But when they rein China's systems back into the global fold, they nonetheless need to protect some critical adaptations of practice in order to keep the focus on what the company needs to do to develop talented people in China—as well as manage them for performance.

Take, for instance, the practice of structuring job grades and compensation. Companies have learned over the years that the two must be both internally consistent with each other and competitive in the market. But in China, the simple truth is that compensation ranges for job bands need to be somewhat broader than they might be in other markets, in order to provide managers with the flexibility they need to reward and motivate talented Chinese employees who learn fast. Chinese employees can come in with different backgrounds and experience levels than, say, expatriates in the same department. Your global systems provide guidance on compensation. But if the Chinese employee learns fast and grows, you want to be able to pay her more to keep her and to motivate her—and because it's fair. It runs against the grain of what you are trying to achieve in China—building a pool of talent—if you are inordinately constrained by narrowly defined job bands.

Recruiting practices require adaptation, too. Many MNCs are less systematic and consistent in their recruiting, screening, and interviewing practices than they typically would be in their operations in Europe or America, and some discipline would help. At the same time, though, HR managers need to shape the process to hire what they need in China—not what the company needs in established markets. That means defining screens, tests, and background checks that prioritize candidates who have demonstrated an aptitude to learn fast, conceptualize the right things, and change and grow.

On the other hand MNCs here have frequently developed HR policies on benefits, promotions, and transfers that are "too Chinese," often linked to their joint ventures. Because most of the investments made in China, particularly early on, came in the form of joint ventures, HR issues quickly became part of the negotiations. Many companies thought that HR was one of the areas where the local partner could add value—after all, they were Chinese! Unfortunately, this meant that salary structures, job promotion tracks, and performance management were tied to the level of the partner's own operations, particularly when the partner was a local state enterprise. Seniority was rewarded over performance. Mobility outside the joint venture was limited. Compensation was restricted by the salary caps of state-owned enterprises. One company executive told us that they had to limit training Chinese executives internationally because "repatriates were not liked by local staff."

High-Performance Culture

Performance management is another critical HR process that MNCs can execute in China as well as they would anywhere else—with largely the same frameworks and approaches—but in a China kind of way. Foreign companies here have underinvested in systems designed to bring out the best in their managers. You typically find spotty adherence to tried-and-true performance management practices common in an MNC's global operations, such as setting clear missions and goals, creating the right organizational structures to support goals, and putting into place good processes for individual and departmental feedback.

This shouldn't be the case. As we researched this book, we undertook a systematic, in-depth study of performance management systems at twenty-four companies in China, including both multinational and local ones, in several industries, including consumer products, industrials, high tech, telecommunications, retail, and financial services. We also conducted less in-depth reviews of several others. We looked at five areas:

1. Does the company have a clear mission and aspiration (understood by employees)?

2. Does it set measurable targets?

3. Has it created organizational structures to support goals?

4. Are mechanisms in place to provide individuals and departments with clear feedback?

5. Does the company hold people accountable for results?

In each of these areas, we looked closely at control levers, such as operating and planning processes, and at motivational levers, such as values and incentives.

We compared what we found in China with a larger McKinsey study of these same factors at three hundred global companies in North America, Europe, and elsewhere in Asia. The top-line finding is that companies with clear and systematic performance management systems deliver better business results than companies that do this poorly.[1] What's worth noting here is that this is as true for companies operating in China as it is for those operating anywhere else in the world, or for those companies' other operations.

In many of the companies we looked at in China, mission statements are vague and targets tend to reflect aspirations rather than come from serious analysis of bottom-up, business-based information. We attended an executive team meeting at one company during which American executives visiting from headquarters spent four hours with their local Chinese colleagues going over every word in a mission statement for the Chinese operations. The Chinese executives were stunned. They had expected a quick review of the statement (which was inordinately vague) and then a move to more substantive issues. The statement that resulted from the meeting, however, was more effective for focusing staff throughout the Chinese operations.

Targets may be set with little rigor, too. Granted, IT infrastructures in China are still dramatically below global standards, making it a challenge to get the data needed to set and measure realistic financial and operational targets accurately. Setting uninformed targets (which may be too low or unrealistically high) and operating with information deficiencies can, in the worst cases, lead managers to make decisions they regret. One textile machinery company invested significantly in new opportunities at the high point of the industry cycle—buoyed by optimism and too little information—only to watch prices for its goods fall by half over the next year or two as local competitors increased capacity. In another instance, the CEO of a multinational company, visiting China, shook hands with the mayor of Shanghai—and soon after his company inked a US$700 million deal with the government without doing a single market study. It will not surprise you that local competitors made mincemeat of the deal.

Yet executives have to set some numbers to get planning systems in motion and provide some prescriptions to the troops. The key is not to let the systems take over. Global planning processes can be very sophisticated, requiring a level of detail unavailable or irrelevant in China. These processes need to be adapted to the Chinese context not by throwing them out, but by recognizing and adjusting the information input needed in order to arrive at the few critical measures that management needs to know. One MNC was surprised to find that the China market had almost doubled versus previous projections, which had been based on global benchmarks and a single base-case forecasting methodology. Since then it has invested in developing scenarios and appropriate levels of investment for each, as well as milestones to check which scenario appeared to be developing.

A related challenge has been simply the hurdle of introducing targets and measures at all in a culture where these things were initially something of a novelty. A large multinational transportation company recently overhauled its systems for capturing and tracking financial and operational information. Essentially, it pared back to a small set of key indicators, let managers get used to understanding the data and hitting targets measured in those systems, and then gradually increased the complexity of the system. Managers' ability to use and manage to more complex performance information increased as well. Essentially, this approach introduced managers to the philosophy of performance measurement and then brought them up the learning curve.

Another MNC has started to tighten performance systems by holding internal performance "Olympics," where plants and sales forces compete against each other on a few critical measures, such as operating costs per unit of output or management of accounts receivable. Again, once the basics are running smoothly, the company can ratchet up the complexity as needed.

Performance also depends on having the right organizational structures in place to allow managers to hit targets. Good execution can be waylaid by unsound organizational structures and reporting lines. At one company we studied, for example, the unit that determined how much of a particular product line the company should buy from Chinese suppliers was not linked to the home country unit responsible for the profit and loss of those lines, and the home country unit had no real incentive to buy more from China. As a result, the China purchasing unit could only grow by buying for other companies as well, and ended up doing one-third of its business for companies other than its own. It was an opportunity squandered by poor organizational design.

It isn't easy to find the right balance of local autonomy and headquarters control of an MNC's China operation, as we've mentioned. Successful global companies consider a matrix of criteria when trying to design the right balance. These criteria include figuring out how to transfer and adapt distinctive capabilities, to exercise operational control throughout global networks, to capture economies of scale across functions, and to develop global-management career tracks.

Timely and unambiguous feedback—another cornerstone of world-class performance management—is rare in China. Some managers in China say providing feedback runs against the cultural grain in a face-conscious society. Yet at the same time, most factory floors in China now prominently feature scoreboards that rate workers according to production and quality. (Apparently only managers have face to lose in China.) We've found good practices at work in a few MNCs in China, and some progressive Chinese companies as well, but they are not the norm. The good practices we've seen include formalized coaching and mentorship programs and processes, and assigning younger managers and professions to shadow more experienced managers, giving the younger people a unique, firsthand opportunity to learn about management with less personal risk.

Local models for good feedback do exist, which we refer to when we talk to managers in China to dispel the notion that feedback will paralyze an organization with fear. Miao Wei, the Party Secretary of Wuhan, developed one such system. Among other things, he is responsible for the evaluation of all government cadres in this city of six million. Soon after he assumed this role, he decided that government would be best served by greater transparency in its evaluation process. He developed performance indicators for every bureau and instituted a regular review process in which he and his senior colleagues could give feedback on their performance directly to department heads. It worked for Jack Welch, and it works for Miao Wei. This level of accountability was an unprecedented step and indicates how far a single leader can take an organization.

Finally, there are rarely consequences for underperformance in China, whether it is being fired or being passed over for a raise or a promotion. The lack of rewards for outstanding performance is just as pernicious a problem. This is a legacy of seniority and state control in many large Chinese businesses (equally a problem across Asia). Many young Chinese managers say they welcome the accountability that comes with responsibility and autonomy, however. They've begun to see in China firsthand the motivational power of doling out rewards for success and triggering consequences for failure. (In some cases the brightest of these young managers have been on the receiving end of "consequence management discussions"—an experience that has helped shape later success.) In Chinese companies such as Lenovo and Ping An, progressive management has brought in these measures, and they have worked. As companies consider how to motivate their employees in China, they must remember that most Chinese employees respond best to systems that tie personal rewards to personal performance.

Multinational companies that came to China but left behind their distinctive performance systems need to get back to basics to win in the decade to come. It's time to adapt the systems to China. Remember how you decided, when you came to China, not to implement the automated sales system that worked so well in America and Europe? Remember how the IT infrastructure was so poor that having salespeople enter data on a laptop computer was, well, a nonstarter? It's time to think again—adapt! For example, one company uses the same principles for its sales systems in China that it uses in North America and Europe, but has simplified the technology. Instead of relying on electronic entry and e-mail submission of sales activities, the firm holds daily or weekly meetings, and all salespeople fill out activity cards on paper.

To win in China, strive for a balance of operational and financial goals. You will need to loosen controls on people anyway—you don't have the information or the infrastructure to run an organization as precisely as you might in the United States. Make use of global knowledge, but set up explicit local measures that are manageable and stick with them.

Of course, this is a tall agenda for executives—particularly given the additional efforts they must make to improve execution in operations across the board, from marketing to product development, and from manufacturing and sourcing to distribution. In the next chapter we look at how executives can get their arms around this broad change agenda effectively.

CHAPTER NINE

Where to Start

As multinational companies start to transform their China operations so that they fire at top-notch level on every cylinder—that is, all critical operating functions and activities—the task can seem daunting. Where do senior executives in China and the home office begin to make changes? Should they begin in marketing or manufacturing, or a balance of both? They should do more sourcing and innovation in China, but with limited resources, which is more important? Who is accountable for changes, and what varied roles do senior executives in the home office and in the China office play?

Of course, there is no magic answer common to all companies in all industries. Nor would a single answer handle all the complexities and uncertainties that characterize the Chinese market today, a market that is in rapid evolution. However, based on our experience working with the companies—both multinational and domestic—that are succeeding at getting things done very well in China, we have found there is a common approach that executives can take to sort though the choices and trade-offs in order to focus on what counts. There is a sequence to sorting through the agenda, from redefining what the global corporation wants to achieve in China—given that all the assumptions a company made when it first went to China ten years ago no longer obtain—to defining China's impact on global strategies.

Like all frameworks, executives get out of it what they put into it. We find these discussions bear most fruit when executives are willing to dig for information, challenge old assumptions, and search for real solutions. As former Honeywell and Allied Signal CEO Larry Bossidy wrote with Ram Charan in their book *Execution: The Discipline of Getting Things Done*, good execution is ultimately "a systematic way of exposing reality and acting on it."[1] To execute well, a company's leaders must assess challenges and opportunities, strengths and weaknesses, with a cold and objective eye and then build a realistic way forward from there.

Set the Agenda

The first step for improving the ability of the company to execute and compete in China is to revisit and potentially reset the management agenda. As we hope we've made clear by now, China is turning a corner, from an emerging market in which companies developed bespoke processes and systems to meet unique operating challenges on a daily basis to a mature one in which competition requires companies to adopt proven global standards for management practice, albeit tailored to fit the local context. The old risks of doing business in China—such as developing the right government relationships, picking the right joint venture partner, and setting up shop in the right city—are being eclipsed by new business risks that are far more familiar to Western executives. The new risks are about competing in an intensely heated atmosphere for a share of the wallets of the largest emerging customer segment in history, in an environment of laws and supply chains and infrastructure that isn't as frontierlike as it once was but isn't as mature as it will be. This environment will always be different from the business landscape in the G8 countries—not only because it is so large, so competitive, and filled with so much unknown potential, but also because of its unique demographics and social and cultural history.

In a market this competitive, companies must play to win, not play to play. In industry after industry, only the leaders will be profitable, and only those who play to win will be leaders. Executives must evaluate their position. If they are in China to win, the first step is to make a commitment to pursuing success and to set the agenda for transformation.

As mentioned in the preface, tens of thousands of foreign and multinational companies are in China, including most of the *Fortune* 500. But multinationals are there in different degrees. Procter & Gamble, Motorola, Yum!, General Motors, Danfoss, and others are there in scale, committed to the opportunity and positioning themselves to be market leaders. (We also believe that *global* leadership will soon depend on winning there.) Others, such as IBM, are starting to make China a significant node in their global operations network, seeing it as integral to the success of their global business strategy. Still other companies aren't so sure: they have assets in China—a toe in the water—and will see how things go. It may not go well if they wait too long to hit the reset button.

Making a commitment to win is, in our experience, a top-down process. The CEO is involved in most cases of success, and typically the board is also integral to the process. Once the corporate purpose is set, the CEO can ask business units and functions to draw the implications as appropriate. At GE, Jack Welch in the early 1990s made it clear, from the corporate perspective, which businesses *had* to be in China, which *might* be in China, and which would definitely *not* go to China. AIG established a first-mover position in China based on CEO Hank Greenberg's personal initiative and drive, which created the opportunity for his Hong Kong leader, Edmund Tse, to build a business there. Likewise, the CEOs of Motorola, General Motors, Danfoss, and other companies directly set the China agenda and then handed it off to business unit leaders to drive it forward.

In all of these instances, moreover, the CEO spent significant time in China to determine priorities. The importance of first-person experience is a recurring theme in this book. Deng Xiaoping described the process of economic reform as "crossing the river by feeling the stones." Just so, successful CEOs come in person to see exactly how different (or not) China is from their expectations before committing to a purpose. In our experience, the turning point for many companies, or for a function within a company, has been a visit to China. A visit by the CEO to see firsthand the vibrancy of China's retail environment or to visit Chinese homes and talk (through a translator) to consumers can be more persuasive than stacks of reports.

Jorgen Clausen, CEO of Danfoss, traveled the old Silk Road and saw his company's future in a provincial city far inland from China's booming cities. Visits to factories and suppliers by procurement heads and factory managers from the United States and Europe can increase the level of confidence an organization has about buying from China—far more so than crates of samples will. Visits with consumers can be illuminating, too. When Bose Corporation's top twenty executives came to China in 2006 to get firsthand impressions of the opportunity, each spent one or two hours in a Chinese household discussing consumer views on audiovisual equipment. Executives were surprised to discover that even in a country with a significantly lower standard of living than the United States, consumers were willing to buy high-end home entertainment products. It made a lasting impression on the executive team.

Set High Aspirations

Once the company's executives have reset the agenda and are committed to competing in China to win, the next, equally critical step toward success is setting the right aspirations. As mentioned earlier, this is one of the fundamental requirements for good execution in China. Winners set the bar high. As golfers say, "100 percent of your short putts can't reach the hole." Companies that win in China set high aspirations for all relevant functions, reward the risk taking required to get there, and are willing to experiment to achieve the goal. Danfoss realized that its double-digit growth in China simply wasn't enough to succeed; market share was the right aspiration. Carrefour established the leading foreign retail business in China totally from scratch, making multimillion dollar bets each time it opened a new hypermarket in cities that most people in France had never heard of before; the company made those bets because executives' decisions were guided by very high aspirations to win in China. P&G realized early on that China would be critical to its global business and set out from day one to be the leader in its product categories against both foreign and local competition. When its momentum threatened to stall in the toughening competitive environment of the late 1990s, P&G redesigned its portfolio, products, and sales and distribution to successfully meet its goal—it did not lower the goal.

A high aspiration also requires much effective blocking and tackling, and top-down support is often necessary to remove barriers and allow space for experimentation. In a survey we conducted recently of forty CEOs of multinational companies, most expressed some level of support in developing their company's China strategy. Among the set of surveyed companies that are winning in China, however, the responding CEOs acknowledged that they had personally involved themselves in resolving issues that arose as impediments to establishing or growing the China business, such as legal problems, budgeting challenges, and HR concerns.

Make Reality-Based Decisions

As these examples suggest, it's not enough just to say you want to win in China. Often you also have to make reality-based strategic choices and trade-offs—for example, which product market to focus on, what kind of factory to build, what distribution structure to develop, and which information architecture to adopt. These big decisions will have a fundamental impact on the business.

Some innovations developed in China—whether products or processes—should be designed to meet local needs and take advantage of low-cost supply or capital expenditure opportunities, as discussed in chapter 4 on product development. But sometimes global consistency can be equally important—for instance, when an innovation designed and made in China becomes a global product. What is important is that the choice you make be based on seeing the reality on the ground, not on popular myths. Honda built its factory in China with substantially less automation than it had in plants in Japan or the United States to take advantage of differences in the capital or labor trade-off possible in China. But in the steel industry, shop-floor labor is a much less important factor in total cost, so Capital Steel is building a vertically integrated automated plant at a pace and scale that astound Western steel executives.

Adapt Global Processes

A dominant theme of this book is that achieving world-class execution means adapting global processes to Chinese reality wherever possible—not creating unique China processes. High-performing MNCs in China bring their global expertise to the Middle Kingdom—the practices, tools, and approaches that have worked elsewhere in their operations. They adapt them where necessary to accommodate local values and culture, work within local constraints, or even take advantage of local opportunities.

Reinventing the wheel on a factory floor makes little sense. Few operating managers in China today would dream of ignoring decades of good experience in Japan, the United States, and Europe when designing production layouts and material flows just because China is somehow different and things ought to be done in a different way. And yet, in other functions, managers do just that. They have been inventing systems and processes since they got to China, and continue to do so even as it becomes increasingly more obvious that bespoke approaches won't help their organizations get to where they need to be in the future.

We've been inside the operations of MNCs in which HR executives have invented their own talent management systems—ignoring completely their company's global systems—because, as they say, "China's cultural traditions are unique and our talent management systems need to reflect that uniqueness." No, they don't. Global systems, with some tweaking, work fine. The bespoke systems, in fact, do not. Talented managers underperform and get raises anyway, or perform well but leave because they do not see a clear development path for themselves. That's not the level of execution MNCs would tolerate anywhere else in the world, and they can no longer tolerate it here.

Institute Global Standards of Excellence

Multinational winners in China also demand a global standard of operating and financial excellence. As mentioned in chapter 1, most substantial foreign entities in China are operating profitably. The annual surveys conducted by the American Chamber of Commerce in China (ACCC) chronicle the steady upward slope of profits over the last decade. Margins are quite good and have been improving: in 2005, 33 percent of ACCC companies had better margins in China than elsewhere in the world. But are they performing as well as they can? As well as they should? As well as they must when competition kicks in with a vengeance?

Ten years ago, companies could dismiss poor performance as the tribulations of an uncertain, emerging market; they weighed outcomes against the strategic decision to be in China. Today they frequently accept good-enough performance, which certainly seems salubrious when it's yielding good margins. However, it's not. The times are changing, and companies that are not gearing up now for the more competitive environment risk losing both their investments to date and their future. Some industries, such as fast-moving consumer goods and consumer electronics, are already in this new era of competition, and only those that prepared well have survived. Nokia's attention to distribution excellence allowed it to withstand the onslaught of domestic phone makers. Yum!'s preemptive brand development is holding up its margins in a toughening retail environment. Carrefour's focus on instituting top-flight supply management and procurement practice, including linking its top suppliers in China to demand information on the mainland and globally, has helped underwrite its leadership position in China—and globally.

Good-enough performance simply doesn't pay well. Substantial money is left on the table when companies don't source all they can from China or pay more than they should for Chinese goods or components. They leave money on the table when waste in their operating plants in China is so prevalent that it is reducing profits by 20 to 40 percent. They are dropping revenues for the taking when they fail to see new market opportunities opening up or when they deliver uncompetitive products to these markets. They are squandering profits when they design products that are more costly to make than they could be, or more costly to deliver than they should be.

Companies should focus not only on the financial numbers but also on the inputs to these numbers, measuring such things as staff turnover and morale in HR, or quality and on-time delivery in manufacturing. Given the labor cost advantage in China, it is possible to deliver short-term financial results at the expense of long-term competitiveness. PLP's China manufacturing plant was growing and profitable, for instance, but was riddled with significant operational problems that the company addressed with a lean overhaul.

Integrate the China Operations Globally

Finally, we believe that, over time, winning companies leverage their success by globalizing their China operation. They rethink

China's role in worldwide strategy, organization, and operations and integrate it globally wherever possible. As China's markets become more competitive, philosophical distinctions are blurring between local companies and multinational companies operating in China. Chinese firms recognize they must get out onto the global stage before multinationals lock them in. Multinational companies appreciate the true ferocity of Chinese entrepreneurialism and hence the importance of beating (or buying) their local competition. The best of both are working to "apply the global standard to China."

This process is iterative. Having decided on a purpose for China operations and gone full cycle through making choices, adapting for the market, and integrating that purpose into the company's global operations, the purpose of the company's China operations should be revisited. It is likely that a China operation that began several years ago as a manufacturing base should now be considered as a base for sales growth and soon for product development for China and the rest of the world. It may have started as a base for low-cost assembly labor and is now one of the sources of global engineering talent. With each turn through the elements of this cycle, the company will get increasing value from China. In a world where China is becoming the center of world manufacturing and is not far from becoming one of the centers of engineering talent and one of the fastest-growing and largest markets, companies that want to win globally will have to develop a mechanism to go through the cycle frequently and with rigor. And they will have to win in China to win in the rest of the world.

To reinforce this last point, in the final two chapters—Part III— we take a look at the future of business in China.

Part Three

The Future
of Business
in China

CHAPTER TEN

The Looming Wave
of Mergers and
Acquisitions

Throughout this book we have argued that multinational companies must dramatically improve how they execute in China, aspiring to achieve world-class levels of performance across multiple organizational functions, if they are to succeed in China's increasingly competitive—and evolving, widening, and growing—markets. They can achieve top-quality execution by adapting proven global managerial practices to the realities of a Chinese context.

But there are two additional reasons why companies here need to become outstanding operators. First, as China's business landscape has changed to become more like everywhere else in the world, the opportunities for companies to buy and merge with each other have begun to expand. We think M&A activity will spike upward over the next decade, potentially reshaping many industries here. Those that can execute well stand a better chance than lackluster operators of succeeding in what we think will become a volatile buying and selling atmosphere.

Second, we believe new managerial standards and practices will emerge in China during the next few years, and companies can adopt these new practices to become more competitive in their operations elsewhere in the world. In a sense, achieving superlative execution in China is all about establishing the platform on which new global standards will be forged. Tomorrow's global winners are those that will soon be quickly creating—and quickly learning how to disseminate globally—the new standards for top-flight execution in China's hard-fought markets.

We will examine each of these issues in turn. This chapter looks at the very different world of mergers and acquisitions in China: both how those that are relatively better at execution stand a better chance of winning at this game, as well as how good execution of M&A deals might appear as this activity begins to heat up. The following chapter looks at how companies might leverage first-rate execution to win in tomorrow's global markets.

Merger Mania

We address the role of world-class execution in merger activity first because it is a near-term challenge for executives. China is on the threshold of a new era in merger activity. Some MNCs will enter second- and third-tier cities, or build scale and gain knowledge in new middle-class markets, by buying their way in. Moreover, the current environment—fraught with overcapacity in many sectors and aggressive price-based competition—is ripe for industry consolidation. Additionally, since the late 1990s, the government has been actively encouraging mergers as a matter of policy, motivated to improve the performance of money-losing state-owned enterprises, consolidate severely fragmented domestic sectors, and foster the growth of potential Chinese champions to rival MNCs on a global stage.

Multinational and domestic Chinese companies are already feverishly identifying the better companies to acquire within their respective sectors. As an added fillip, many MNCs are also starting to buy their joint venture partners. With ten to fifteen years' experience in China and greater freedom to operate as businesses on their own, these MNCs believe they can acquire their way out of legacy arrangements that no longer add value. And within the last two years most of the major multinational private equity firms have begun to raise funds to hunt for opportunities in China.

Although the real frenzy of M&A activity lies ahead of us, momentum has been building over the last few years. The rate of company acquisitions and mergers has been rising at about 20 percent a year since the late 1990s, and the growth in the value of those deals has been growing at a 25 percent annual clip. In fact, mergers and acquisitions accounted for as much as 20 percent of all foreign investment in China in 2005.[1] One year later, McKinsey estimated that the number of major M&A deals in 2006 had nearly doubled over the previous year, accounting for 32 percent of utilized foreign capital in China.[2]

As M&A activity heats up in China, companies will face the same strategic choices they face in this regard anywhere else in the world. Can they buy markets by buying companies that serve them? Can they gain scale advantages? How about better control over sector pricing? Can they rationalize capacity? Are there advantages to forward or backward integrating their value chains?

Can they change the competitive dynamics of their sectors? These, and a host of other game-changing questions that executives ask as they contemplate potential acquisitions (or real or potential transactions by competitors) in any market in the world, will be questions that executives in China must ask and answer also. In developed markets, successive waves of M&A activity have broadly narrowed these considerations. In China, everything is just opening up—the strategic possibilities affected by mergers are far more open and less defined, and probably a great deal more volatile among and across sectors.

In other words, as M&A activity begins to heat up, it is already clear that everyone will have to play and that the game will become very intense in some sectors. Executives of MNCs had better fasten their seat belts, because M&A will be one wild ride in China. The lack of good data and market intermediaries makes it difficult to identify good acquisition targets—you're driving in more fog than would envelop you in deals in the developed market. Making deals work often requires a complex restructuring of assets you would not have to do elsewhere in the world. You have to determine the value of the deal with more guesswork. And the Chinese regulatory environment fosters a great deal of noneconomic M&A behavior that will bewilder Western executives and complicate a multinational company's M&A plans.

It can be done successfully, however. In July 2004, Belgian brewer InBev (formerly Interbrew, prior to its merger with Brazil's AmBev) acquired a 70 percent equity stake in Zhejiang Shiliang Brewery Company for US$53 million. The acquisition boosted InBev's market share in Zhejiang province, one of the wealthiest regions in China, to 50 percent and provided a distribution network in the province that InBev could leverage to advance sales of other products. It also gave InBev a strong local brand: Red Shiliang beer. Finally, InBev gained a good management team

(Zhejiang Shiliang was profitable, with margins fatter than some other domestic rivals), good equipment, and an organization open to adopting the operating improvements InBev would bring in. Three years later, it is clear that by all measures the acquisition has been a success.

Eventually, as China's M&A market matures, deal making in China will come to resemble deal making in the world's other centers. But that time is a long way off. To understand why, it is worth highlighting the broad realities of mergers in China today.

The Landscape for Mergers and Acquisitions

Multinational companies transacted few acquisitions in China until the late 1990s. Prior to that, MNCs faced an uncertain and daunting legal environment for M&A, and, more important, there was simply very little to buy. Local governments still protected the big state enterprises, and the private sector was a mosaic of small firms with limited assets. The government began to dismantle the hurdles to M&A at the turn of the century. In 1994, the State Economic and Trade Commission began to encourage Chinese and foreign investors to purchase money-losing state-owned enterprises in eighteen pilot cities, sweetening the deal by offering generous loan restructuring terms and providing subsidies to help clear bad debts.

At the same time, changes in China's regulatory system, legal environment, and financial markets began to make acquisitions possible. For example, although legal institutions are still in their embryonic stages, there is sufficient precedent in M&A cases now for parties to major transactions to feel more confident that the courts will enforce their contracts. Also, government officials have become more business savvy when deciding among bidders for an enterprise: today, decisions are far more likely to be made based on the business advantages that a purchaser can offer rather than on the personal relationships between government officials and bidding companies or the political stature of the bidders.

The pool of acquisition targets has improved, too. China's state and private enterprises have grown rapidly in recent years. As China's markets have expanded, so too have its companies' fortunes, which have been invested in assets, technologies, and brands that in turn have made them more appealing acquisition candidates for MNCs. Even when the investments these domestic companies made have turned out to be financially disastrous for their shareholders, acquirers (foreign or domestic) may still find the companies attractive targets. For example, Michelin purchased Shanghai Tire in 2001 primarily to take advantage of the excellent radial tire-making equipment Shanghai Tire had invested in but was unable to productively employ. Moreover, when the investments do turn out right, they can form the basis for an acquisition platform. Some domestic companies have been among the most aggressive acquirers in China. Hainan Airlines, for example, leveraged its Haikou base to become the fourth-largest airline in China through the acquisition of Changan and Xinhua Airlines.

Still, there remain some structural barriers to M&A in China—particularly if a multinational company is looking to buy a Chinese company listed on one of China's exchanges. The state still controls over 60 percent of the average listed company's equity, in the form of nontradable shares. Transactions of listed companies therefore still depend on the whims of the state equity holders, reducing transparency in the market for corporate control. Also, prices quoted for China's listed companies are inflated by international standards. As of this writing, the market has been very volatile. Valuations have soared, and many commentators worry that the mainland markets are in a bubble. Prices do not seem to be driven by economic fundamentals, as they might be in larger developed markets, in part because of the huge pent-up demand for equities and because retail rather than institutional investors dominate these markets—and there is a lot of speculating going on.

For a prospective buyer, the implication is that the prices demanded for listed entities in China often bear no relationship to their cash flow. This also means that investors able to control a listed vehicle may take advantage of access to the domestic capital markets to fund buying sprees. The management of otherwise bankrupt listed companies can preserve themselves simply by continually raising funds from stockholders who are keen to speculate on growth and lack investment alternatives other than bank deposits. In this environment, M&A of listed companies remains difficult to achieve.

But even this isn't a barrier to smart deal making. One private equity firm used the purchase of a listed company as a platform for consolidating the cement industry in one of China's provinces—gaining a return seven to eight times its investment in just five years. The investors saw the cement industry as open to provincial-level consolidation. Their first step was to invest in a listed cement company, purchasing nontraded state shares as well as a portion of the floated stock. This equity allowed them to provide management with significant incentives to improve their operating performance, accompanied by an infusion of management know-how. As a second step, the private equity firm acquired majority interests in smaller cement businesses that were close to the listed company's businesses and that met the industry consolidation rationale. Their total production capacity increased from 400,000 to 1 million tons, and operational performance further improved. At the same time, they had the listed company issue 350 million renminbi in new shares to raise capital for further acquisitions and for equipment upgrades. Finally, they sold the smaller firms to the listed company, consolidating 90 percent of the province's high-quality cement market. The price paid for the smaller firms on their resale to the listed company, plus the rise in value of the listed company from the industry consolidation, delivered the investors a 700 percent return.

As we look forward, we expect market-driven M&A deals to take off like a rocket. The government is likely to encourage this. Domestic industry consolidation is now spreading to the more capital-intensive sectors of the economy, including automotive components, steel, and machinery. Capital markets reform could accelerate this trend—the government has announced its intent to reduce its share of listed companies from 60 percent to 33 percent by 2008. The formation of pension funds and deregulation of insurance companies to allow them to invest in the stock market will also introduce a new class of more disciplined, value-oriented investors.

Making Deals Work

Success in M&A deals in this environment favors those companies that already have their operations in world-class shape. Consumer product companies will need to make a number of transactions in local markets, for instance. Knowing clearly the road map for products, segments, and region—the marketing analysis we suggested in chapter 3—is a useful basis for determining what you need for your portfolio, where, and why before starting to screen potential targets. Groupe Danone, for instance, is rolling out a targeted strategy for growth in wider circles in China through local brands—and has acquired more than three dozen Chinese companies to get there.

Companies that have implemented lean or other improvement programs in their manufacturing operations are better positioned to improve their acquisition targets and capture the value of an acquisition faster. Alcoa, for instance, purchased Kaiser's manufacturing assets in China. Alcoa used the knowledge and experience gained from overhauling its own operations in Shanghai to quickly turn the Kaiser assets around. Today, Alcoa's China operations are some of its best performing in the world.

Similarly, being top flight at execution in management of distribution gives a potential acquirer greater flexibility to consolidate supply chains, transform distribution networks, or swap poor-performing suppliers or distributors for better ones. And acquisitions potentially provide access to good talent. If the acquirer has done its homework and put in place world-class systems and processes for developing talent and managing for performance, the talent is more likely to stay and help the acquirer grow.

But being in fit shape to make smarter decisions about what companies to buy and why—and to be positioned to integrate acquisitions more quickly and effectively—isn't enough. Companies also will have to become first rate at each of the capabilities necessary to execute M&A transactions in China to get value from them. Just as increasingly fierce competition in China demands outstanding performance in marketing, product development, manufacturing, sourcing, distribution, and talent management worldwide, so too the same Darwinian logic will apply to M&A transactions. Similarly, the global best practices that MNCs have in place in their developed markets to identify and screen acquisition targets, structure and negotiate deals, conduct due diligence, and integrate the acquired operations will apply in China as well—if adapted to the very different situation.

It isn't yet clear what these new China-colored global practices will look like. It's too soon to say. However, we can delineate some of the China-specific differences that MNCs will encounter in their M&A pursuits, and suggest the general shape of how practices will need to be adapted to be world class in China. Let's look at a few of the key steps.

Screening Targets

Doing deals in China used to be simple: the government told you with whom you could partner, and you said yes or no. Today, deal opportunities abound. In addition to state-owned enterprises, there are a fast-growing number of private Chinese companies that MNCs can purchase, and some MNCs in China are looking for a way out and are selling off their ventures here.

Assessing and prioritizing opportunities can be challenging in China, however. It can be tough to get information on potential acquisition targets, or even enough information to know what the full field of potential targets might be. Also, because the field of possibilities changes rapidly, static lists don't stay relevant for long. For instance, many MNCs put serious effort into identifying potential joint venture candidates when they first arrived in China. Some of these companies tell us they are using these lists as a starting point for forward-looking M&A targeting. Based on what we have seen on those lists, however, the degree of reevaluation needed to make them useful is substantial. The competitive situation is in such rapid flux that some companies they thought highly of when they first arrived here have stumbled, whereas others have subsequently engaged in joint venture partnerships with later-arriving foreign companies.

So where do companies begin? They can employ a wide range of sources to develop target databases, just as they might elsewhere in the world. For instance, in addition to the usual sources— published information and articles, government and market reports, local analyst reports and research studies—a few MNCs are interviewing distributors, suppliers, customers, local market consultants, and industry observers for additional ideas for developing a preliminary roll call of potential targets. It works in Europe and America, and it works in China, too. A few MNCs have also established processes to glean target information from their sales forces. This could be particularly effective in China because the need for primary data is so much greater. Rich information from the field on customers and competitors can help merger teams better sort good acquisition targets from bad ones.

But too few MNCs take advantage of another deal-identifying asset that is more specific to China. Simply being in China and willing to play in the deal flow, making acquisitions or publicly assessing potential targets, and building credibility concerning action are steps that attract information about deals that companies might not be able to get otherwise. Emerson Electric, Siemens, and InBev have all found this to be true, now that their appetites for local market acquisitions are becoming common knowledge in business and government circles. Other MNCs could follow suit. Local governments are approaching MNCs because the central government is pushing the municipalities to divest ownership interests in local government-owned companies. Local governments are not primarily interested in the cash generated by these deals, but rather in extinguishing liabilities for large workforces and capital assets, allowing for very favorable deal structures (see the following section).

There are other practices companies can adopt to improve their screening capabilities here. Some MNC executives in China have asked their staff to cull potential targets by applying China-specific filters in their assessments. For instance, they've learned that scale assessments in China aren't what they are elsewhere. If a target lacks a minimum size and position, acquiring it will yield little tangible benefit over starting out on one's own. That's true anywhere, of course, but in China, what constitutes minimum may be lower than elsewhere. One machinery industry MNC has figured out that companies with revenues as low as US$5 million can add value, whereas the cutoff for its targets in developed markets are companies with US$20 to US$50 million in revenues. The Chinese companies they are buying have had a higher growth potential than companies in more developed markets.

For similar reasons, smart MNCs—such as the equipment maker just mentioned—also dig deeper into an assessment of the target company's customer base than they do with potential acquisitions elsewhere in the world. In B2B sectors in China, the speed at which the target company's customer base is growing is a good barometer of the target's growth prospects, especially if customers say that they view the target as a long-term supplier of their critical needs.

Structuring the Deal

In China, foreigners have four basic choices regarding how they invest in an acquisition. Almost all acquisitions by foreigners in China require the formation of a foreign investment enterprise (FIE). The typical investment approaches companies have adopted are either forming equity joint ventures with a Chinese partner (a theme that has several variations) or creating wholly foreign owned enterprises. These approaches afford the greatest legal protections available. But there are two other possibilities: Companies are also establishing regional holding companies to pull together multiple acquisitions under one organizational roof and to consolidate tax losses, legally share services across businesses, and enhance their relationships with local governments. A holding company cannot take the place of an FIE but can optimize its setup. Finally, MNCs also structure deals as offshore special-purpose vehicles (SPVs). An SPV is an investment approach that does not require the formation of an FIE, and allows a purchaser to acquire or dispose of shares of domestic entities held in another SPV without government jurisdiction and review. Companies seeking to consolidate multiple ventures in China find this an attractive option.

Looking ahead, we think MNCs will increasingly prefer to structure deals to buy assets—factories, for instance—rather than take equity stakes. There are drawbacks to buying assets. Most Chinese companies have a lot of noncore assets, stemming from a history of diversification. They also have social responsibilities to their workers, including housing, health, and education commitments. Separating these assets from the seller's broader organization can be a time-consuming effort and often involves a multinational buyer in separate negotiations for each asset (i.e., each asset and liability requires separate legal transfer). Supplier and customer contracts end and have to be renegotiated. The purchaser may also not be able to use the corporate or business identity of the target and has no access to its net operating losses.

However, several benefits of asset ownership outweigh these costs and complexities. For instance, in an asset deal the acquirer is not liable for any future target liability, which can be hard to determine even with the most thorough due diligence. Moreover, the acquirer can use target assets as collateral for takeover financing. This implies that these deals will require a much more detailed due diligence than is typically true in the United States or Europe, where corporate equity transactions are the rule.

The deal structures that MNCs may utilize over the next decade are to some extent being colored by the activity in which they are engaged today. Many MNCs in China today are restructuring joint venture deals they signed during the last decade or so. Under Chinese law, either side can make it difficult to break up, requiring government approvals that may be difficult to obtain.

The trick, then, has been for MNCs to develop deals that are win-win for both partners. A number of M&A deals in the future, therefore, will be opportunities created as these legacy partnerships unravel. How these legacy partnerships will unwind could vary. Private local investors will be very unwilling to part with their stakes in profitable businesses, even if they have long ceased to add any value to the partnership (as Yum! apparently is finding). Majority partners may be able to exert pressure on their counterparts to sell by withholding products or technology, essentially forcing a closure. One MNC acquired the assets of a partner in this way.

Sometimes creating a win-win proposition to reach closure on a partnership can look more like the flat side of a blunt instrument. In 2001, Alcatel successfully restructured its joint venture with a subsidiary of China's Ministry of Posts and Telecommunications by presenting its partner with a stark choice. The joint venture dated to the 1980s, when Alcatel bought a 40 percent stake in a venture that had a 70 percent share of the telecommunications equipment market. By the late 1990s, however, the venture's technology was lagging, and new entrants such as Cisco and aggressive local companies such as Huawei were coming on the scene. As a minority investor, Alcatel was unable to exercise management control or set the technology road map. So, Alcatel went to the Ministry of Information Industry (MII) with a proposition: restructure the venture or see it gradually go under. After extensive discussions, the MII agreed and sold 10.1 percent additional equity—and management control—to Alcatel for US$312 million. Alcatel injected new proprietary technology to strengthen the business's competitiveness. China has since become one of Alcatel's largest markets, with over US$3 billion in sales in 2003, including exports of US$1 billion.

Performing Valuation Under Uncertainty

In developed nations, valuation has become something of a science, but in China it is still more of an art. Public market trading values are not reliable guides. The domestic stock market is highly volatile and provides a huge premium to domestic companies, given the largely retail investor base and the high volume of speculative trading. Transaction multiples are equally dangerous to rely on given the relative scarcity of deals and the typically high premiums paid. With less than fifteen hundred annual transactions in total (and less than three hundred transactions internationally), there are limited benchmarks for investors to use. Finally, regulators require that state assets be sold at no less than 90 percent of their net asset value, as certified by a state asset appraiser. This last requirement does not necessarily determine values of private companies and may also be subject to interpretation, depending on how anxious the state agency is to sell the asset.

The most adept merger managers at MNCs in China tell us they avoid overly rigid use of discounted cash flow (DCF) valuations. Good DCF valuations rest on regulatory and competitive assumptions about the future, which is a tricky business in China, where the former can be opaque and the latter highly volatile. Instead, these executives say their companies use immediately tangible cash flows as the primary basis for valuation, and adjust only for economic shifts that they see will have a major and immediate effect—within, say, the next two years.

In one recent industrial acquisition, the target company was forecasting that prices would decline steadily, as they had for the past few years. But the acquirer saw that looming overcapacity would have a dramatic impact on industry pricing. It based its analysis on the cash costs of the marginal players and on previous industry behavior, and revised the price forecast to reflect a one-time drop. On this more realistic basis, the acquirer negotiated a price that was within its limits, making the difference between a go and no-go decision—a smart move, as it turned out.

Conducting Due Diligence

Conducting due diligence on a potential acquisition is a core activity of an M&A group in any multinational company. But M&A specialists will need to adjust many of the proven analytical methodologies they use in developed markets to the realities of China today if they are to get a real sense of the opportunities at stake. In their walk-throughs of potential targets, they will encounter business practices that remain antiquated after decades of state control. If specialists were to find these practices in operation in a factory in Germany, it would not be good news, but in China it is more typical news and should be weighed accordingly. Similarly, the standard analyses of channel evolution and segmentation that specialists can conduct in developed nations are more difficult to do because of a general lack of information; the target company may not even have management forecasts. A lot of expected data simply does not exist. Because IT systems are weak, databases lack breadth and capacity.

Mergers and acquisitions staff will need to learn to work around these limitations—but also will need to assess the target with an understanding of its potential relative to other choices in China, not relative to potential targets in developed markets. Similarly, they will need to assess legal risks through a China-specific lens. Legal systems and requirements remain inadequate and opaque. Few agreements are documented, and enforcement of contracts is ultimately determined by reference to principles of precedent, fact, and (importantly) fairness. Even core agreements that a target company made may be oral, and numerous cash deals are hard to substantiate, so investors will have to anticipate greater liability and risk exposure. This will be particularly true in agreements with related parties, such as employment and raw materials supply or tax agreements with local government.

World-class execution of due diligence activities in China will likely involve teams with the resources to dig deep for business and operational information. We've noticed, for instance, that a few companies in China have recently recruited accounting and legal advisers with local experience into their due diligence teams. Others have staffed due diligence teams with people based in the area where the target company is located who have a track record of doing business locally, presumably giving them insider knowledge and a network of relationships that will enable the team to understand the workings of the target company. Although theoretically teams can gain a high-level understanding of a company fairly quickly, in our experience with companies doing deals we've noticed that significant findings tend to emerge over time (e.g., regarding financial structuring issues), meaning that it can sometimes take months to fully understand a company's situation. Best practice in China requires that teams take their time to do the job right.

Many things are different in China, and all bear investigation by due diligence teams, including land use rights (land is owned by the state) and tax liabilities. But here are four unique problems we think will shape the practice of due diligence in China:

- *Tracking asset ownership*—Chinese companies often form with inadequate documentation as evidence of their assets. This issue becomes even more troublesome if the company has involved many related parties, because Chinese companies often acquire assets through bank borrowing and pledge the acquired assets as security. Such practices can pose a further problem because the system for registering mortgages and pledges in China is poorly developed and implemented. First-class due diligence teams in China will need to develop effective practices for confirming the ownership of assets, investigating related companies to understand the business and financing transactions between the target company and its related companies, and ascertaining whether acquired assets are subject to a bank pledge.

- *Leased brand names and trademarks*—Companies may not actually own some intellectual properties even though they use them regularly. Teams investigating ownership should make no assumptions—and leave no stone unturned.

- *Asset and employment conditions*—World-class teams should take pains to verify the true value of the reported equipment of Chinese companies. They also need to understand the real work of employees, given a tendency for excessive employment in state-owned enterprises. One multinational company M&A team considers individual productivity a key component in its due diligence efforts, and therefore determines the real number of people the target enterprise employs.

- *Licensing*—Articles of incorporation and business licenses typically allow for organizations to operate within a very narrow business scope. Certain specialized lines of business require licenses from government agencies, and Chinese law does not always allow the transfer of licenses in M&A transactions. Moreover, foreign ownership may affect applications for, and renewals of, licenses. Top teams need to make sure that the target company is authorized to conduct the business it's in, and that the MNC can transfer the licenses to the merged entity.

Managing the Merger

The most difficult part of any acquisition is merging the two organizations once the deal is done. Countless studies of mergers in developed markets have shown that the majority of acquisitions fail to deliver value, and that the reasons for these failures can frequently be attributed to how the merger was executed rather than how the deal was valued and structured.

The story will no doubt be the same in China. World-class execution of merger integration in China will largely resemble practice found in developed markets. Yes, there are integration challenges in China that are unique. For instance, merging an acquisition will be complicated by culture. People do not work across functions in Chinese companies, so adapting best practices that involve cross-functional teams will take some trial and error. Also, the quality of management will complicate adaptation of merger-integration best practices. For instance, departmental responsibilities are typically ill-defined in Chinese companies, resulting in a lot of buck passing both within and between departments that can cripple efficiency. Goal setting and accountability are rare, performance systems are inadequate, and so on. Global practice will need to be tailored in each instance.

Yet despite these differences, the principles of good post-merger management apply as much in China as they do in developed markets. When you look closely at some of the successful mergers in China, you find the same few factors determining success as you do anywhere. Senior managers commit to making the merger a success, agree on what success is, and speak with one voice as they exhort the troops forward. The local or global CEO (depending on how big the deal is) plays a visible role. Managers establish clear expectations for change—key performance indicators. They take a step-by-step approach, breaking big objectives down to smaller ones, and start with the easy initiatives to get some fast wins. They foster a spirit of ownership within the company, use role modeling, and put high performers on the merger integration team. All this is familiar to multinational managers who have the experience in making and integrating deals elsewhere and can rely on that experience in China.

One difference, however, is governance. Multinational companies usually gain full control of an acquired company. There are many reasons why they would want full control of an acquisition in China, too, including a desire to replace Chinese managers in whom they may not have confidence, a need to consolidate earnings, and a drive to simplify governance. However, Chinese target companies and their government partners share an equal desire for control. Also, the Chinese government prohibits foreign control of companies in twenty-five industries. Moreover, even when a partner is amenable to ceding governance control, the joint venture company is typically structured as an operating unit of the parent organization, whether government or private, and the owners of the parent organization make the investment decisions. There is limited transparency in those decisions and a lack of commercial and financial know-how. As a result, governance is a critical element of success in executing M&A deals in China.

When the acquirer secures a majority ownership, it typically gains majority power on the board and appoints management. Serial acquirers such as ASIMCO Technologies, a foreign-owned auto parts company, change management quickly and efficiently after a merger. They don't allow bad apples to stick around to create an atmosphere of suspicion and distrust that can take years to overcome.

But governance is a more complex issue when regulations limit the investor to a minority equity stake, as in financial services, the automotive industry, and energy. A few MNCs have secured some measure of control in these kinds of transactions by securing a presence on the board that reflects the economics of transaction (and the law in China) and by obtaining a say in the election of independent directors. For instance, in one fifty-fifty joint venture, the MNC investor succeeded in nominating three of the nine board members directly, selecting and approving three independent directors, appointing the vice chairman, establishing and nominating executive committees, and gaining control and oversight of key functional tasks (such as finance and marketing).

In other instances, companies have traded with Chinese owners to gain control of functions that count to the MNC. For instance, one high-tech investor appointed the chief financial officer to control accounting and have full access to performance management systems (inaccurate accounting and fraud is a major concern for foreign investors). The company also appointed the chief technology officer to ensure technology upgrades. What was the trade-off? The MNC's Chinese partner got to appoint executives to the top operations and HR positions as well as to appoint the general manager.

Still another approach some MNCs have tried is to get their Chinese partners to agree to processes and mechanisms that have the effect of delivering control of key strategic and operational decisions to MNC managers in the operations. In the insurance industry, one minority foreign investor persuaded its Chinese owners to establish a surprisingly high threshold for board approval of investment decisions (where the investor lacked control), thus keeping those decisions at the operating management level (where the foreigner had control).

Another tactic might be to extract explicit shareholder rights that require consent for key decisions. For instance, the acquisition deal could stipulate that senior management hires, capital increases, budgeting, dividend policies, investments of a specific scale, or asset sales must be subject to minority investor veto rights. Or foreign investors could negotiate for step-up options that entitle the foreign investor to increase its ownership percentage under a pre-agreed formula, assuming the regulatory environment allows this. Chinese financial investors may even be able to provide offshore collateral to put in escrow against the risk of default.

It isn't yet clear if any of these approaches—or combinations of them—are best practices for merger governance in China, or if some other, far superior practices will emerge. The innovation that will happen in M&A management in China lies ahead. Trying, learning, adapting, and trying again will be the rule in mergers as it has been in all other aspects of execution in China.

CHAPTER ELEVEN

Win in China–
or Lose Everywhere

To win in the rapidly changing environment of China, organizations need to learn the right ways to evolve to stay in the lead. Most immediately, they need to learn how to reach emerging customer segments with new products. Selling global brands to affluent customers in top-tier cities taught MNCs quite a lot about China (and helped China learn about how to engage in global markets for capital, trade, labor, and exchange). But capturing share with customers in China's emerging, and massive, middle class in cities that differ from a marketing and channel perspective (and will differ as far as profitability is concerned, too) is largely an unknown adventure. Information and insights are scarce now; capturing them systematically will be difficult for the foreseeable future. In the interim, companies will make the best judgments they can, and smart companies will closely monitor and analyze results.

They also need to learn how to execute well to win in China's intensely competitive environment. That means taking proven practices, processes, tools, and frameworks that work elsewhere—global standards—and adapting them to the China context. But this is a temporary gambit. These adapted practices will quickly evolve in this competitive hothouse. And some of what is currently uncertain about markets and products will become more certain.

Take innovation, for instance. China is large enough to both draw in global companies and let weaker local firms stay in business. That leaves the market severely fragmented, with too many factories making too many products, and prices are plunging.[1] To survive, companies must innovate in both operations and product development. The world's leading companies are competing head-on with China's own, both taking advantage of the world's lowest cost structures. This phenomenon is occurring nowhere else to the same magnitude. The companies and products that emerge from that competition will be well placed to win with customers anywhere.

The example of Galanz offers a glimpse of the future. Galanz, a Chinese company, is the world's largest manufacturer of microwave ovens. It first looked at the market in 1991 and judged microwave penetration in China to be about 5 percent at the time, compared with 80 percent in most developed markets. Japanese and European companies claimed that 5 percent. Galanz entered the market, matching the foreign brands on performance but hammering them on price—slashing prices by 80 percent over five years to 2002, and making microwaves affordable to an ever-increasing market of buyers.

By 1995 Galanz had 25 percent of the market in China, and by 1998 it had 61.4 percent. The next year, Galanz started to sell units in the United States. Sales soared to 18 million units by 2004, triple what they were when Galanz entered America. By 2002, Galanz had a 40 percent share of the global market, with a 45 percent share in Europe and more than 70 percent in South America and Africa. Galanz has since started to compete in markets for air conditioners and rice cookers, aiming to be the world's largest manufacturer of these items by unit volume by the end of 2007. Its China-based designs are quickly eating into global markets, both emerging and developed.

In other words, the twenty-first-century business model for nearly every industry is cooking on the stove in China. Companies that learn faster than rivals how to innovate and compete aggressively in this white-hot environment—whether they are MNCs or local—will achieve winning positions in China and eventually will win in global markets as well. Having the capability to learn how to evolve the new global standards in China, how to identify new practices quickly and move them into the company's other operations around the world, how to market with new tools discovered in a tough and ambiguous environment, and how to source, design, and manufacture in China for domestic and global markets is a calculus for success that companies may need to have sooner than they think.

Imagine the global economy in ten or twenty years. How many Chinese companies will be in the *Fortune* 500—not just because they are big but because they are excellent? How many top executives in the leading European and American companies will have risen from the ranks of the company's Chinese subsidiary into positions of global leadership? How many products selling in the United States and Europe will have been developed in R&D centers in Shanghai, Beijing, or even cities situated deeper in China's heartland? The answers to these questions are potentially staggering.

In 1985, when the personal computer was a fairly new product, few could imagine that in just ten years Taiwanese companies would be assembling most of the world's PCs, and in twenty years not only assembling them but also designing some of the PC's most important parts—including the semiconductors, which are also made in Taiwan. Few, too, could imagine just how disaggregated the sector's value chain would become—and how efficient that disaggregating would be.

Where might this evolve? Today, notebook computers are largely made in China and shipped around the world by air—something that can be done because their value is high enough and the units small enough that the cost of air freight is manageable. Desktop computers, however, are more bulky and command lower prices, so they are assembled near the market where they are sold—frequently in Mexico for North America, in eastern Europe for Europe, and in China for Asia. But what if part of the PC could be made in China and assembled on board a large vessel as it transports the product to its destination market? Or what if some significant part of the PC were made and assembled in China, and more time-sensitive parts were added closer to the customer? How does the value chain change if China becomes the world's largest, or second-largest, single market for personal computers?

Take another sector: retail. Retailers have been buying goods in Asia since the 1970s, and apparel factories began to move east with increasing momentum during the 1990s. Today Wal-Mart would be China's fifth-largest trading partner if the retailer were a country, and many other retailers are not far behind. In the apparel sector, design capabilities are now starting to shift to China. How far this will go, and how fast, is unclear. The only thing clear is that economics are continuing to drive the importance of China in this industry.

To push this point, consider the insurance industry. Construction materials are available from China at a significant discount from their cost in the United States. And yet as of the time of writing, most insurance companies still use subcontractors to repair homes and cars, and these subcontractors are buying their materials at local hardware stores and do-it-yourself stores and through local parts distributors. Imagine the value to a major insurance company of buying direct from China, reducing the cost of materials by 20, 30, or even 50 percent, putting a portion of that savings into the required distribution network to get the materials to the subcontractors, and then sharing the rest in part with consumers through lower premiums and in part with shareholders through improved earnings.

China is fast becoming the world's factory. Lean and Six Sigma approaches are just starting to take root there. But when they become common practice, and lean-savvy managers develop innovations on the factory floor—new approaches to reducing cost and improving quality and cycle time—will MNCs be able to capture what's learned and transfer new best practices to plants elsewhere in Asia, or in South America, the United States and Europe, Africa, and the Middle East? What practices did Galanz develop to produce a microwave oven that global customers love at one-fifth the cost of rivals?

China is a megatrend, with the potential to reshape global competition, sector by sector, in ways we cannot yet imagine—but can begin to learn. The learning will have to take place in China itself, in the heat of competitive battle. But lessons will only be learned and shared throughout the company, if executives proactively build into their operations the incentives and mechanisms to experiment and learn.

In the years to come, the phrase "applying the global standard to China" may evolve to "developing the global standard in China." For many functions, what works well in China will increasingly influence the global standard. Despite the intensity of China's markets, MNCs are investing more and more there. And they are not just placing large, capital-intensive bets. Apart from manufacturing, the investments are in sales, marketing, and product development. In the technology sectors in particular, significant R&D centers across China are developing product first for China and then for world markets. They are banking on China's increasingly talented, low-cost, and very deep pool of technical skills. China is already setting product and market standards in consumer electronics and automotive components. As other industries mature, the world will view China as a premium source of industrial talent and capabilities.

We believe, as China merges into the global economy, best practice in China will become best practice globally and vice versa. Given the scale of its markets, a preferential share of China will deliver a global structural advantage. More products developed in China will become global standards, in industrial processes as well as consumer goods. The ability to develop a Chinese talent pool will therefore be critical across all functions. Astute execution in China will deliver a telling worldwide advantage, one that companies cannot afford to concede.

NOTES

Chapter 1

1. McKinsey Global Institute, "From 'Made in China' to 'Sold in China': The Rise of the Chinese Urban Consumer" (San Francisco: McKinsey & Company, November 2006), www.mckinsey.com.

2. McKinsey Global Institute, "From 'Made in China' to 'Sold in China.'" See also, Diana Farrell, Ulrich A. Gersch, and Elizabeth Stephenson, "The Value of China's Emerging Middle Class," *McKinsey Quarterly* (2006 Special Edition: "Serving the New Chinese Consumer"), 60–69 (www.mckinseyquarterly.com).

3. See, for instance, Z. John Zhang, "How and Why Chinese Firms Excel," in "The Art of Price War,'" Knowledge@Wharton, December 2006, http://knowledge.wharton.upenn.edu/index.cfm?fa=viewarticle&id=1625.

4. Unpublished McKinsey research, 2006.

Chapter 2

1. See David O. Becker, "Gambling on Customers: An Interview with Harrah's CEO, Gary Loveman," *McKinsey Quarterly* 2 (2003), 46–59 (www.mckinseyquarterly.com).

2. See Stephen J. Dorgan, John J. Dowdy, and Thomas M. Rippin, "The Link Between Management and Productivity," *McKinsey Quarterly* (February 2006).

3. Ibid.

4. Private conversation between executive and authors.

Chapter 3

1. Comments by Jorgen Clausen throughout this chapter are from notes from a Fall 2005 discussion between Clausen and our McKinsey colleague William Hoover. For an edited version of the discussion, see

William Hoover, "Making China Your Second Home Market: An Interview with the CEO of Danfoss," *McKinsey Quarterly* 1 (2006), 84–93.

2. The center has conducted a number of analyses of the data and conducted other research on Chinese consumer preferences and buying behaviors. For a fuller look at these studies, see "Serving the New Chinese Consumer," *McKinsey Quarterly* (2006 Special Edition).

3. Notes from a conversation between Chereau and our McKinsey colleague Peter Child. An edited version of this conversation was published as "Lessons from a Global Retailer: An Interview with the President of Carrefour, China," *McKinsey Quarterly* (2006 Special Edition: "Serving the New Chinese Consumer"), 70–81 (www.mckinseyquarterly.com).

4. McKinsey China Consumer Center conducted in-depth interviews with six thousand individuals in households in more than thirty large and small cities throughout China during 2006 and 2007. The data complied from these interviews—analyses and additional interviews are ongoing—provide insights into Chinese consumer attitudes and behaviors.

5. Ibid.

6. This phenomenon is not confined to China. Marketers in some fast-moving consumer goods businesses have noted a rise in similar consumer behaviors in developed markets, such as western Europe. It may be that the explosion of product categories, marketing messages, and marketing channels in developed markets is prompting an increase in last-minute decision making by buyers in stores and restaurants.

7. Ad Avoidance Survey, Lowe & Partners Worldwide.

Chapter 4

1. McKinsey research, 2006, not released publicly.

2. Private conversation between executive and authors.

3. Notes from a Fall 2005 discussion between Clausen and our McKinsey colleague William Hoover. For an edited version of the discussion, see William Hoover, "Making China Your Second Home Market: An Interview with the CEO of Danfoss," *McKinsey Quarterly* 1 (2006), 84–93 (www.mckinseyquarterly.com).

4. It's worth noting that countries have historically tightened enforcement of IP protection once they have companies with IP to protect. Britain strove to protect industrial "copying" by Americans in the late eighteenth and early nineteenth century, and the United States stepped up enforcement of software piracy once it had a software industry to protect.

5. These issues are discussed in greater detail in O'Melveny & Myers, LLP, Q&A on Intellectual Property Law in China (Beijing: O'Melveny & Myers, LLP, August 2006). We would also like to thank Lester Ross, co-managing partner of the Beijing office of WilmerHale, and Grace Chen, an IP specialist at WilmerHale, for their help in developing insights on the management of IP in China.

6. However, progress is being made on this front. In a recent landmark case here, one Chinese company took another to court for hiring away employees who took IP with them. As more domestic companies turn to the legal system for IP protection, enforcement will increase.

Chapter 5

1. James R. Hexter, "Better Manufacturing in China: An Interview with Two of PLP's Top Executives," October 2006 (mckinseyquarterly.com). All quotes from PLP executives in this chapter are from the interview.

Chapter 6

1. General Motors, for instance, ships engines made in China to assembly plants in the United States and Canada, and is selling some China-made Chevys in Russia and Chile, but this is just a start.

2. Comments by Diane Long in this chapter come from notes of discussions about sourcing issues that one of the authors had with Long.

Chapter 7

1. Nokia entered China in 1985 and started selling mobile phones in 1994, and Sony Ericsson entered China in 1978 and started selling mobile phones in 1995.

2. The government long prohibited 100 percent foreign ownership of wholesale and retail operations. Today, with the exception of some sectors—such as chemicals or books—this is no longer the case for businesses structured as wholly owned foreign enterprises. This change, which began at the end of 2004, is partly why we see so many multinational retailers buying out their joint venture partners today. Some restrictions still remain, however, which limit a foreign company's ability to compete freely, such as restrictions on the number of dealerships a foreign company can have.

Chapter 8

1. McKinsey has developed a large database of organizational and performance information on these five "performance ethic" levers, as well as numerous control and motivational levers used in hundreds of corporations worldwide. For more information on the findings of these studies see Keith Leslie, Mark A. Loch, and William Schaninger, "Managing Your Organization by Evidence," *McKinsey Quarterly* 3 (2006), 65–75; and Aaron De Smet, Mark A. Loch, and William Schaninger, "Anatomy of a Healthy Company," *McKinsey Quarterly* Web Exclusive, May 2007 (www.mckinseyquarterly.com).

Chapter 9

1. Larry Bossidy and Ram Charan, *Execution: The Discipline of Getting Things Done* (New York: Crown Business Publishing, 2002).

Chapter 10

1. The Chinese Embassy in the United States (citing FDI and cross-boarder M&A figures reported in the United Nations World Investment Report) calculates the number to be nearly 20 percent in 2005.

2. Unpublished McKinsey analysis of M&A transactions in China, 2006.

Chapter 11

1. It is beyond our remit in these pages to discuss why overcapacity is prevalent in China, but the fact remains that it is. See the McKinsey Global Institute's reports on China's financial systems for more information, www.mckinsey.com.

INDEX

adidas, 116
advertising in China, 62–63
AIA (American International
    Assurance), 39
AIG, 162
Alcatel, 184
Alcoa, 94, 179
American Chamber of Commerce,
    5, 123
ASIMCO Technologies, 190
asset ownership, 187–188
Audi, 65
auto sector
    distribution system, 130
    innovations, 70–71
    marketing strategy example, 65
    potential to expand sourcing, 109

Baosteel, 94–95, 101
Bossidy, Larry, 160
brand names, 188
brands in China
    consumer preference for
        domestic, 58–60
    loyalty to, 63–64
    names and, 188
Bright Dairy & Food Company, 63

Capital Steel, 165
Carrefour China, 53, 120, 163, 167
Caterpillar, 138

channel schemes. *See also*
    distribution
    need for, 132
    strategies, 134–135
    system evolution examples,
        133–135
Charan, Ram, 160
Chereau, Jean-Luc, 53
Chery Automobile, 79–80
Citigroup, 147–148
Clausen, Jorgen, 47–48, 78, 162
clean-sheet costing, 121
compensation, 146–147
consumers. *See also* markets in
    China
    consumer evolution in China,
        20–22
    preference for domestic brands,
        58–60
    segment expansion by P&G, 6–7
    segments, 47–48, 50
    strategies for appealing to
        middle class, 61–62
copyrights. *See* intellectual
    property
customer service opportunities,
    137–138

Daewoo, 138
Danfoss, 47–50, 55, 78, 162, 163
Deng Xiaoping, 15, 162
design institutes, 76–77

design-to-cost (DTC) practices, 7,
77–78
distribution
channel schemes, 132–135
customer service opportunities,
137–138
distributors' basic functions, 136
financing opportunities, 138–139
financing risks, 139
infrastructure challenges, 27–28
MNCs' execution challenges,
27–28
partnership mind-set, 139–141
partnerships, 135–137
regional differences in logistics
of products, 52–54
sector example (*see* mobile
telephone sector)
state of current system, 130–131
typical MNCs setup, 126–127
DuPont, 69

equity stakes for IP protection, 86
Estée Lauder, 69
*Execution: The Discipline of Getting
Things Done* (Bossidy and
Charan), 160

fast-moving consumer goods
(FMCG), 140
financing and distribution,
138–139
foreign investment enterprise
(FIE), 182

Galanz, 194–195
GE China, 42

General Agreement on Tariffs and
Trade (GATT), 80
General Electric
adaptation of supplier audit
process, 119–120
commitment to win, 162
competitive advantage in hiring
and retention, 147–148
financing solutions, 138
IP safeguards, 85
manufacturing standard, 94
sourcing strategy, 111–113
General Motors, 80
government relations/regulations
current evolving situation,
16–17
focus of successful companies,
18–19
government's efforts to end
corruption, 17–18
intellectual property and, 87
overall government
involvement, 18
past situation, 15–16
post-merger governance, 190
regulatory system changes for
M&A, 175–176
structural barriers to M&As,
176–177
Groupe Danone, 178

Haag, Bill, 90, 92
Haier, 23, 24, 70, 137
Hainan Airlines, 176
Honda, 164
HSBC, 147–148
human resources (HR) and MNCs
benefits of working for an
MNC, 145–146

compensation and, 146–147
competition for local talent,
    144–145
competitive advantage in hiring
    and retention, 147–148
hierarchical mind-set, 28–29
knowledge of staffers and
    sourcing, 115
needed systems adaptations,
    150–151
need for knowledgeable local
    people, 143–144
people management, 38–40
performance management (*see*
    performance management)
recruiting practices, 151
standards among MNCs in
    China, 148–151
talent management success,
    28–29
talent management systems, 165
"tight on people, loose on
    controls" goal, 149
Hyundai, 138

IBM, 69, 112
InBev, 174–175
infrastructure
    challenges in China, 27–28
    markets and, 47
innovations
    in the automotive sector, 70–71
    competitive advantage and,
        194–195
    national policy to encourage, 81
insurance industry, 196–197
intellectual property
    company responsibility for,
        82–84

concerns about protection,
    79–80
enforcement of rights, 80–81
government relations and, 87
legal action regarding, 84–85
mind-set of people in China,
    80
national policy to encourage
    innovation and, 81
patent registration, 84
protection strategies, 85–86,
    87–88
pyramid, 83

Johnson & Johnson, 77, 134

kaizen events, 99
KFC, 10. *See also* Yum! Brands
Kongfu Spirit, 63

labor costs and manufacturing,
    89–90
lean techniques
    adopting and implementing,
        92–95
    capital costs and, 103
    communications and training,
        102–103
    knowledge base development,
        97–100
    performance culture creation,
        100–101
    pilot projects use, 102
    sustainable gains goal, 101–103
    time frame involved, 103
licensing, 188–189
Li Ka-shing, 3–4

linear performance pricing, 122
Long, Diane, 116, 118, 123

managers and staffers. *See* human
    resources (HR) and MNCs
manufacturing
    labor costs and, 89–90
    lean techniques use (*see* lean
        techniques)
    operations example, 90–93
    plant improvements needed, 92
    supply management (*see*
        sourcing)
    systems needed, 96–97
    waste prevalence, 91–92,
        95–96
    waste reduction benefits, 96
markets in China
    advertising, 62
    brand loyalty, 63–64
    consumer preference for
        domestic brands, 58–60
    customer segments, 47–48, 50
    fluidity of the environment,
        64–65
    future of China, 197–198
    infrastructure improvements,
        47
    innovation and aggressive
        competition, 194–195
    market data collection, 57–58
    market data quality, 56–57
    market research challenges,
        73–74
    MNCs' marketing challenges,
        50–51
    product-by-segment-by-region
        consideration imperative,
        54–56

product development (*see*
    product development)
product performance
    requirements unique to
    China, 48–49
regional differences in
    products, 52–54
sales growth versus market
    share, 49–50
sector possibilities, 196–197
strategies for appealing to
    middle-class consumers,
    61–62
susceptibility to point-of-sale
    pitches, 61
word of mouth and, 63
McKinsey and Company
    China Consumer Center,
        20–21, 52, 58, 62
    McKinsey Global Institute, 20
    research, 24, 32, 61, 69, 96,
        152–153, 173
mergers and acquisitions (M&A)
    business fitness and, 178–180
    current environment, 172–173
    deal structuring, 182–184
    due diligence, 186–189
    history in China, 175
    integration challenges, 189
    local presence advantage,
        181
    opportunities for, 176
    post-merger governance,
        190–192
    rate of, 173
    regulatory system changes,
        175–176
    scale assessments, 181–182
    strategic choices, 173–174
    structural barriers, 176–177

success examples, 174–175, 177–178
success factors, 189–190
targets screening diligence, 180–182
valuations, 185–186
Miao Wei, 156
Michelin, 176
Microsoft, 69
microwave ovens, 194–195
Mittal Steel, 5
MNCs (multinational companies)
  economic growth challenges, 5–6
  emerging technologies and processes, 14
  execution challenges in China, 8–10
  getting started in China (*see* strategy for getting started in China)
  globalizing China operations, 14, 42–43
  government relations (*see* government relations/regulations)
  impact of moving R&D to China, 71–72
  investments in China, 69–70
  involvement in China, 4–5
  key challenges (*see* MNCs' execution challenges)
  refocusing of business in China, 50
  research centers in China, 69
  strategies for appealing to middle class consumers, 61–62
  talent management (*see* human resources (HR) and MNCs)
  typical distribution setup, 126–127

MNCs' execution challenges
  business-to-business markets, 25–27
  distribution and infrastructure, 27–28
  hierarchical mind-set, 28–29
  local competition, 22–24
  logistics, 10
  marketing, 50–51
  profile of the Chinese consumer, 20–22
  rising costs, 24–25
mobile telephone sector
  competitive picture, 125–126
  domestic companies' tactics, 127
  Nokia's adaptations, 128
  system challenges, 128–129
  typical MNC distribution setup, 126–127
Motorola, 4–5, 68

Ningbo Bird, 127
Nokia, 60, 126, 127–128
Novartis, 5, 60, 69, 80

partnerships in China, 135–137, 139–141
patents. *See* intellectual property
performance culture, 100–101
performance management
  elements of, 152
  feedback and, 155–156
  mission statements and, 153
  MNCs' challenges, 28–29
  organizational structures and, 155
  reward systems, 156–157

performance management
  (*continued*)
  targets-setting discipline,
    153–154
personal computer industry,
  196
pilot testing, 79, 102
Pizza Hut, 10, 13. *See also* Yum!
  Brands
poka yoke, 94
Preformed Line Products (PLP),
  5, 90–93, 99
Procter & Gamble (P&G)
  adaptation of supplier audit
    process, 119–120
  aspirations for China, 163–164
  customer segments expansion,
    6–7
  design-to-cost approach, 7
  distribution system's evolution,
    133–134
  focus on consumer preferences,
    60
  marketing strategy, 4
  market research, 74
  market share in China, 3
  partnership approach, 3–4,
    140
  product development group,
    74–75
  product testing, 79
  spending on advertising in
    China, 63
  successful R&D practices,
    72–73
  success in China, 55
product development
  China-specific automotive
    innovations, 70–71

  China-specific design
    allowance, 78
  cost containment through
    relaxed specifications, 75–76
  design-to-cost practices, 77–78
  focus on low-cost in design,
    76–77
  impact of moving R&D to
    China, 71–72
  intellectual property issues (*see*
    intellectual property)
  investments by MNCs, 69–70
  maintaining standards for, 75
  market research challenges,
    73–74
  operational oversight required,
    78–79
  performance requirements
    unique to China, 48–49
  pilot testing, 79
  premium versus generic
    products, 77–78
  product-by-segment-by-region
    consideration imperative,
    54–56
  R&D by a foreign company
    example, 68
  regional differences in
    products, 52–54
  research centers of MNCs, 69
  successful practices, 72–73
pull systems, 94
pyramid, intellectual property,
  83

quick service restaurant (QSR)
  industry, 10–11. *See also*
  Yum! Brands

R&D. *See* product development
retail industry, 196
Roche, 80

Samsung, 5, 135–136
Shanghai General Motors (SGM), 70
Shanghai Tire, 176
Siemens, 138
Six Sigma, 94
sourcing
    global best practices use, 118
    global standards adaptation, 119–122
    impediments to increased, 109
    knowledge of staffers and, 115
    lack of high aspirations for, 107
    levels possible, 109, 110–111
    on-site management and design teams use, 116–117
    oversight importance, 122–124
    potential to expand, 106–107, 109
    procurement cycle times reduction, 113–114
    scope of, 108
    setting as a corporate goal, 114–115
    strategy examples, 111–113
special purpose vehicles (SPVs), 182–183
strategy for getting started in China
    commitment to win, 161–162
    execution (*see* world-class execution principles)
    first-person experience importance, 162–163

global best practices and, 165–166
global integration of China operations, 167–168
global standards of excellence and, 166–167
making reality-based decisions, 164–165
overall environment, 160–161
setting aspirations, 163–164
supply management. *See* sourcing

talent management. *See* human resources (HR) and MNCs
teenagers and brand loyalty, 64
television as an advertising medium, 62–63
Toyota, 118, 141
trademarks, 188. *See also* intellectual property
Tse, Edmund, 162

Wal-Mart, 5, 32
word of mouth and consumer markets, 63
world-class execution principles
    adapting versus adopting global practices, 34–35
    cross-industry adaptability, 31–32
    globalizing China operations, 42–43
    making readjustments, 37–38
    measuring learning, 40–42
    people management, 38–40
    quality of execution linked to financial performance, 33–34

world-class execution principles
(*continued*)
research on adopting best
practices, 32–33
setting aspirations, 36–37
World Intellectual Property
Organization (WIPO), 80
Wu Yu, 90, 99

Xian Janssen Pharmaceutical,
134

Yili, 63
Yum! Brands
challenges in China, 10–11,
166
growth and profits, 13
operating capacity building,
11–12
operations unique to China,
12–13

Zhao Zhouli, 95

ABOUT THE AUTHORS

Jimmy Hexter is a director of McKinsey & Company and leads the firm's Operations Practice in Asia. He is located in the Beijing office and speaks fluent Chinese. In his fourteen years with the firm, he has served multinational and Chinese companies in many industries, particularly on operations strategy, manufacturing performance, and procurement and supply chain strategy. He has published extensively in the *McKinsey Quarterly*, the *Asian Wall Street Journal*, and other publications, and is a frequent speaker at executive events, such as the American Chamber of Commerce in Shanghai Annual Procurement Conference, where he was a keynote speaker in 2004 and 2005. Jimmy is a graduate of the Harvard Business School, where he was a Baker Scholar and received the Thomas A. Wolfe and Henry Ford awards.

Jonathan Woetzel is a director of McKinsey & Company and a co-founder (in 1986) of the firm's China office. He has led McKinsey's China Corporate Finance and Asia Energy and Materials practices. In his twenty-two years with the firm, he has served a broad range of Chinese and multinational companies on strategy and operations, M&A, governance, and other management issues. He is also an adviser to the Joint U.S.–China Coalition for Clean Energy. His previous books include *Capitalist China: Strategies for a Revolutionized Economy* (2003) and *China's Economic Opening to the Outside World: The Politics of Empowerment* (1989). Also, he has authored or coauthored numerous articles in the *McKinsey*

Quarterly, the *Asian Wall Street Journal*, *South China Morning Post*, and other publications. In 2005, *Consulting Magazine* named him one of the top twenty-five most influential consultants. Jonathan holds a PhD in political science, and speaks fluent Chinese, Spanish, and German. He lives in Shanghai with his family.